Praise for *The Execution Factor*

Practical and must-read advice. This book is exactly what the next generation of entrepreneurs needs.

—BILL SHAW, President, Entrepreneur Media

The Execution Factor should be read by all entrepreneurs or anyone looking to take their career to the next level. Pay attention and take notes—this book is a blueprint for success.

—JAMES BOROW, Global Director of
Product Strategy, Snap, Inc.

The Execution Factor is for the entrepreneur in all of us, for the person daydreaming about being their own boss while stuck at a nine to five. Kim Perell knows what it takes to execute a vision, no matter how big or small. There isn't a better book to guide you to turning your ideas into reality.

—CHRIS BURCH, CEO of Burch Creative Capital
and cofounder of Tory Burch

Since meeting Kim I have always been in awe of her entrepreneurial successes. This book is a great distillation of all of her years of experience and the learnings she has gathered along the way. If you're an entrepreneur, an executive, or someone just starting their career this book is a must have.

—ERIC TODA, Director of Marketing at Gap, Inc.

The Execution Factor serves as your personal coach for mastering the one skill that sets successful entrepreneurs apart from others—*execution*. This book should be on every entrepreneur's shelf, whether you're starting a company or launching a side hustle in your living room.

—FRAN HAUSER, former president of digital at Time, Inc.
and author of *The Myth of the Nice Girl*

Kim Perell has written a very personal and compelling guidebook on entrepreneurship, how to execute with excellence, and on the importance of resilience. It's an extremely readable, powerful, and personal narrative that I would highly recommend to all aspiring entrepreneurs. I already have a dozen people in mind with whom I'm going to share this work.

—JONATHAN AUERBACH,
Chief Strategy and Growth Officer at PayPal

If you're intentional about upskilling or upgrading, *The Execution Factor* gives you the framework and traits to get there. Through her own wealth of examples and applicable process, Perell has created essential reading that cracks the code on how to drive success in your life and work.

—ERICA GOLDEN, Global Talent Development at Apple, Inc.

Whether you're a seasoned entrepreneur or just launching your career, you will benefit from the insights and inspiration in *The Execution Factor*. I wish I had this book when I was starting out.

—KEITH FERRAZZI, *New York Times* bestselling
author of *Never Eat Alone* and *Who's Got Your Back*

An easy read with many great takeaways, Kim nails the process of becoming a successful entrepreneur with her five traits of execution. Kim is her own force of nature, and this book will help you make your own path to success crystal clear.

—MEL ROBBINS, author of *Kick Ass* and *The 5 Second Rule*

As a venture investor and advisor to large corporations I work with entrepreneurs and intrapreneurs on a daily basis. Kim Perell's book provides practical and must-read advice to every aspiring and experienced entrepreneur.

—EVANGELOS SIMOUDIS, PhD,
cofounder and Managing Director of Synapse Partners
and author of *The Big Data Opportunity in Our Driverless Future*

Kim Perell is a SPARK—she recognized early on that there are dreamers and doers in this world, and she is undoubtedly a doer. If you're seeking to get ahead, read *this* book. It shows you that success isn't happenstance. You must work for it, and she shows you how.

—ANGIE MORGAN and COURTNEY LYNCH,
New York Times bestselling authors of *SPARK*

Everyone we admire took action and executed consistently to achieve their success. Kim is right: Visualization without action is delusion. This book will help you execute on the yellow brick road to your Oz.

—KEITH J. CUNNINGHAM, founder, Keys to the Vault
and author of *The Road Less Stupid*

To succeed in business you must be able to execute. Kim's book *The Execution Factor* provides the right strategies to get things done.

—STEPHEN KEY, bestselling author of *One Simple Idea*

THE
EXECUTION
FACTOR

THE ONE SKILL THAT
DRIVES SUCCESS

KIM PERELL

NEW YORK CHICAGO SAN FRANCISCO ATHENS
LONDON MADRID MEXICO CITY MILAN
NEW DELHI SINGAPORE SYDNEY TORONTO

1 2 3 4 5 6 7 8 9   LCR   23 22 21 20 19 18

ISBN 978-1-260-12852-9
MHID   1-260-12852-0

e-ISBN 978-1-260-12853-6
e-MHID   1-260-12853-9

Library of Congress Cataloging-in-Publication Data

Names: Perell, Kim, author.
Title: The execution factor : master the one skill that drives success / Kim
   Perell.
Description: 1 Edition. l New York : McGraw-Hill Education, 2018.
Identifiers: LCCN 2018016819l ISBN 9781260128529 (hardback) l ISBN
1260128520
Subjects: LCSH: Success in business. l Motivation (Psychology) l BISAC:
   BUSINESS & ECONOMICS / Motivational.
Classification: LCC HF5386 .P4727 2018 l DDC 650.1—dc23 LC record available at
https://lccn.loc.gov/2018016819

McGraw-Hill Education products are available at special quantity discounts to use as premiums and sales promotions or for use in corporate training programs. To contact a representative, please visit the Contact Us pages at www.mhprofessional.com.

*For my Dad and Mom, two of the greatest
entrepreneurs I know.
I couldn't have asked for better parents or role models.*

Contents

Letter to the Reader   xi

1. Hitting Rock Bottom: The Truth About Success   1

T R A I T   1

VISION

Your North Star

2. Moon Shot   29

3. Living Someone Else's Dream   37

4. Don't Just Think It, Ink It   49

5. The Loneliest Trait   57

Vision—Trait Summary and Real-Life Scenario   65

T R A I T   2

PASSION

What You're Willing to Sacrifice and Suffer For

6. What We Do for Love   69

7. Emotional Rescue   77

8. Fueling Your Fire   89

9. Never Completely Submit to the Dark Side   103

    Passion—Trait Summary and Real-Life Scenario   109

TRAIT 3
ACTION
Taking That First Step and the Next One

10. Setting the Stage to Act   113

11. Prioritize Action: Better to Start Than
     Procrastinate   121

12. Vision Quest   131

13. Fear of Flying   145

     Action—Trait Summary and Real-Life Scenario   159

TRAIT 4
RESILIENCE
Dealing with Obstacles, Change, and Uncertainty

14. Life Rarely Goes as Planned   163

15. Bouncing Back After Setbacks   171

16. Fail Forward   175

17. Minds and Hearts   179

18. Practicing and Preparing for Resilience   189

     Resilience—Trait Summary and Real-Life Scenario 201

TRAIT 5
RELATIONSHIPS
Having the Right People in Your Life

19. The Human Touch   205

20. Life Is a Team Sport   215

21. Audit Your Life   233

22. Sharing Your Success   247

   Relationships—Trait Summary and
   Real-Life Scenario   255

Conclusion: Creating an Execution
Blueprint for Your Success   257

Acknowledgments   259

Notes   261

Index   263

The road to success is always under construction.

—ANONYMOUS

Dear Friend,

When I started my first company 15 years ago, I was broke, unemployed, and trying to convince anyone to lend me money was an uphill battle. Thankfully my 80-year-old grandmother made a bet on me.

My goal is to pay her generosity forward by investing in entrepreneurs who need someone to believe in them. And I believe in you.

I am so confident that if you master execution, you will increase your chances of success that I have created The Execution Factor Fund to help you and other entrepreneurs turn your dreams into reality.

The Execution Factor Fund will provide seed stage funding in execution-led startups, providing early financing to entrepreneurs and connecting them with industry experts. I am so grateful for the success I have had, I am personally providing the first $1 million to the fund, plus I am contributing 100 percent of the royalties from this book.

Are you ready to execute your vision and turn your dream into reality? Then apply to The Execution Factor Fund! For more information on The Execution Factor Fund and how to apply, please visit KimPerell.com.

Let's get started, together!

Kim

1

Hitting Rock Bottom: The Truth About Success

've been broke twice in my life. The first time was August 1, 1998.

OK, I wasn't *totally* broke. I had exactly $366.42 to my name. That was the amount listed on the balance sheet I showed my parents as part of a presentation to ask them for a loan before starting my senior year at college.

Yes, a presentation. I couldn't just *ask* my parents for money. Everything in our family had to be worked for. If I ever complained to my dad about a long day at a job, he'd say, "Eight hours? That's a half day." Those words weren't meant to be negative; they were meant to be *motivating*, and I took them that way.

Growing up, if we didn't have and couldn't earn what we needed, we looked for other ways to solve problems—usually around the same kitchen table I was using to make my loan presentation. While other families talked about sports, school, or politics at the dinner table, our conversations revolved around the ups and downs of business—often from very different perspectives. My parents were both entrepreneurs, but they were cut from very different entrepreneurial cloth.

My mother is all heart. She built a consulting business working within companies on their vision and values. They hired her to help them with team building and to understand how to put people before profits. While she has been relentless in her pursuit of business, constantly reinventing her work, even pivoting to take on new kinds of companies as clients, my mom's career has for the most part been and remained stable.

My father? He's the complete opposite. He's a vision guy—a serial entrepreneur who sees opportunity everywhere. He has a degree in engineering from Columbia University, but he has never looked for an engineering job. When my parents arrived in Portland, Oregon, over 40 years ago, he had another vision. Or should I say, many—sometimes too many. First, he pursued his vision for a self-service auto repair garage where people could rent tools and space to fix their own cars. Then, when the market for that failed to appear, he took an offer to help fix a roofing plant and ended up creating a machine to make roof tiles. When the housing market bottomed out, he shut down the tile business, and he made deals with the banks to take over foreclosed homes for pennies on the dollar, refurbish them, and flip them. After that, he started a restaurant, a bar, and got into the elder care business . . .

Most people probably would have given up the entrepreneurial life if they had faced bankruptcy as many times as my dad had. But not my dad. He never gave up. He was always working toward something, and he never stopped believing that success was always waiting for him, just around the corner. And many times it was. As a result, there were times we had more than we needed and times we had almost nothing, when anything that wasn't absolutely necessary was a luxury. Like heat.

One winter our house was so cold that we layered up until our arms stuck out like gingerbread men. Our old wood fireplace was no match for the glacial temperatures. One especially frigid night, the cold got to me so I went to find my dad to tell him. No surprise, I found him buried in his massive old coat working in the garage. When I walked in, he turned, looked down at my fearful face, and before I could speak, he gave me a kind smile.

"We're OK," he said. "We're tougher than this."

And I . . . went back inside and continued to bundle up.

Today I can see the value of having two parents who are entrepreneurs, especially in the way they raised me. Even at the lowest points, they believed in themselves. They committed themselves body and soul to the futures they dreamed of for our family. And they were tough as nails. Tenacity was a tenet I was brought up on. If going a winter without heating was the price of success, then we were willing to pay it—together.

Today I know that makes me one of the lucky ones. The ability to dream abundantly, combined with a willingness to put in the necessary hard work, conditioned me well to overcome setbacks, hard times, bankruptcy, and just everyday things that didn't swing in my favor. It's hard to beat a person who never gives up and has the grit and determination to be bigger than the challenges ahead. I always rise to the occasion. I'm exacting and relentless, which elevated my pitch for a loan before going back to my senior year in college.

Making a successful pitch for anything that satisfied my dad's head and my mom's heart was a challenge, but I was ready and determined to state my case. They listened as I explained my situation. I started by telling them how grateful I was that they had paid for my tuition. This was no small feat for two entrepreneurs who had worked hard for everything we had and expected the same from my brother, twin sister, and me. Reviewing my itemized expenses, I reminded them I had worked all through college to pay for my housing, food, and all my other needs. I had not been wasteful or irresponsible. I was just a broke college kid who needed some extra funds to make it to the start of school after using the last of her savings for rent. I would get a job and pay them back as soon as I went back to school.

"I'm a safe bet for an investment," I concluded.

After some discussion, I got the loan. Or should I say, I earned it. With the loan secured, the conversation took a sharp turn to my future.

"What's your vision for yourself after graduation, Kim?"

Mom wanted me to get a stable job at an established reputable company. That's all she ever wanted for me: to be true to myself, follow my dreams, and be happy.

Dad wanted me to be happy too. However, he didn't want me to take any job where there was a limit to what I could control and how much I could earn.

I felt as most college kids did: overwhelmed and confused. I didn't know exactly what I wanted to do or what I saw for myself.

At that moment I was sure of only one thing: being broke and now in debt to my parents, I wanted to make a lot of money. Not being able to repay their generosity wasn't an option. Investment banking seemed like an appealing option as two of my uncles worked for Merrill Lynch at the time. I also liked marketing.

I excelled in both subjects in school, but I knew I still needed to learn more about them in the real world.

That fall, I did some schedule Jenga and arranged to have classes on two days and to work on the other three: 6 a.m. to noon at an investment bank and afternoons at a marketing company. I loved the marketing work, but I probably would have ended up in investment banking had not one thing happened that pushed me into a career I hadn't much considered: Yahoo!

Yahoo! had gone public while I was in college, and by the time I graduated, the dot-com boom was reaching a fever pitch. All of a sudden, there seemed to be opportunities and money everywhere. It was thrilling. It was a gold rush, and the Promised Land was the Internet. The frenzy was impossible to resist. I ended up accepting a job as a marketing analyst at a dot-com—the seventh hire at a startup in Los Angeles. The company was a kind of 1990s precursor to Dropbox. I was there when we raised our first million and when we raised $120 million more in venture capital shortly after. Things quickly grew exponentially in the office, and we expanded to more than 300 people. I oversaw the entire Internet marketing and sales division. At 23, I had 30 people reporting to me, many of them close friends and people I knew from college whom I wanted to share the opportunity with.

I became a dot-com millionaire in company stock. I was on top of the world. It didn't last. Our biggest issues were timing, volume, and pricing. Data storage costs were expensive back then, and we needed to find a way to offset our burn rate. I took the initiative.

As I saw my father do when he failed, I scoured for any opportunity for survival. That's when I realized we had millions of subscribers for free data storage that we could monetize in a different way. I knew from my work senior year in marketing that those subscribers were worth something to advertisers. So I started to call advertising agencies to see if they were interested in advertising to these subscribers. Overnight, we moved our customer services reps to digital sales reps. We managed to generate more than $9 million in advertising revenue in the first 10 months.

The problem was that we weren't an advertising company. And we still weren't sustainable as a data storage company. My team's ad revenue was the only revenue stream we had, and it wasn't nearly enough to keep us afloat.

Then in March 2001, the dot-com bubble burst, and my company went bankrupt. I had to lay off all my colleagues and some of my dearest friends (some of whom did not talk to me again for years). They had bet on me. They had trusted me. I had failed them. When I was done laying them off, the company fired me too.

In an instant, it was as if someone pushed the delete button on my career, professional identity, and future—not to mention my income. Our stock was worth nothing. In a moment, everything I had worked so tirelessly for had vanished.

At 23, I was unemployed and broke *again*.

Rock Bottom Makes You Realize What You Want

I have never felt worse than I did in the days and weeks that followed. Having let my team go and being let go myself, I soon became more determined to never, *ever* feel that way again. I had loved my job, the company, and my team. I was devastated. Simply put, I had failed people who depended on me. I vowed to shift my thinking and build something on my own that wouldn't have that same outcome and to create the life I wanted.

But what did I want? I made a list:

> Freedom
> Be my own boss
> Control my destiny

I knew exactly where to start to get these things: where I left off.

While the company I worked for was hemorrhaging cash, my division was generating revenue. I was growing advertising revenue even as the company crashed. The Internet was still growing at a bewildering pace. Millions of new people were getting online, and companies wanted to reach them. I knew there must be opportunities in digital advertising, especially for those businesses that didn't need or couldn't afford a large advertising budget.

What they needed was me, and to start again, all I needed was a computer, an Internet connection, and my experience and relationships to leverage.

But while I had the knowledge and the relationships, I didn't have a place to live and work or the money to buy the computer and get online. Love solved the first problem: My boyfriend at the time was born in Hawaii. His parents said if we could get there, we could live rent free in their condo for three months. My family solved the other problem: I borrowed $10,000 from my grandmother with promises to pay every dollar back as soon as I could.

Within weeks, we were off to Hawaii—the magical land of endless surf and sand, palm trees, and bright beautiful flowers across lush mountain vistas—to start my first company.

Aloha! A-*NO*ha!

There was nothing vacation-like about my move to Hawaii. My new business took over the small condo from the kitchen to the living room. My desk was the black marble surface of the kitchen table island that extended from the counter. Wires and cables for the computer and phone dangled like tentacles over the side. We tucked the printer and fax into a nook next to the coffee maker. Boxes and stacks of paper sat on the stove. I could have easily been distracted by the draw of the sun and outdoor adventures with my friends, but I stayed focused on growing my company and the life I wanted—*needed*—to create.

The only talk about the beach came from the voices of my boyfriend's sister and her friend blasting MTV six feet away from me in the adjacent room talking about how great the island was.

Oh, there was one more thing: I was scared. No, I was terrified. I may have had entrepreneurs for parents and some experience in digital advertising, but that didn't mean I knew what I was doing. The part of me that is most similar to my mother is that we hate uncertainty; the part of me that is like my dad told me to *keep going* despite the fear and risks—to persevere just the way we did in those long cold winters.

And I did.

I sat and worked at that table every day for nearly three years straight. Eventually, I hired a small team. I frequently stayed up all night working, taking 8 a.m. calls from the East Coast at 2 a.m. island time. I soon learned that in Hawaii, this kind of drive and ambition tended to be seen as an anomaly. It was grueling and beachless. While everyone left work when the surf was up to find the best waves, I surfed the Internet looking for business opportunities. When the market for digital advertising dried up, I persisted and looked for consumer products that I could source directly from manufacturers to sell online. I bought and sold products ranging from toys to teeth whitener. I did everything I could to keep things going. I maxed out my credit cards to make payroll.

But I never lost faith. Never lost control. Never forgot how great it felt to be my own boss. Never took my freedom for granted. During this time, I also got engaged to my boyfriend. I asked him for a super-long engagement, but he thought the eight years we had spent dating was long enough. He was right, so the following months I started planning our wedding. Each day went something like this: work, work, invitations, work, dress fittings, work, work, wedding planning. I scrupulously budgeted and tracked for the wedding the same way I did for the company across many spreadsheets. And it all paid off: I married the love of my life, and my digital marketing company was growing.

My company expanded as the online advertising market grew and the demand for pay-for-performance advertising proved to be a growth opportunity for digital companies. Within a few years, we had generated over $3.5 million in revenue with 63 customers and five employees. Each year after, we doubled our revenue. We outgrew not only the kitchen but also Hawaii, and we moved back to California to be closer to my husband's family in San Diego.

Five years into growing the company, something happened that changed everything. I was having lunch with a friend who also owned an Internet advertising company, and he told me he was going to sell it. I thought to myself, *Maybe I should do the same.* I hadn't intended to sell my company when I started it. My only goal was to meet my three conditions of satisfaction—freedom, be my own boss, control my destiny—and have the life I envisioned. The sleepless nights, the stress of having employees, and the 16-hour workdays had added up, and selling the company would give me time to fully secure and maybe even enjoy my financial freedom.

I hired KPMG and put the company up for sale. In 2008, I sold it for $30 million, including a two-year earn out. I stayed on as its CEO, retained all my employees, and hired more to sustain our growth.

Broke at 23, I was a multimillionaire by the time I was 30.

With my financial freedom assured, I also became an active angel investor to help other entrepreneurs achieve the same success. As of 2018, I had invested in over 70 companies, 14 of which have successfully been acquired by the likes of Apple and Intuit. One company I invested in was valued at over $1 billion on the first day of its IPO.

Today I live the extraordinary life that I had imagined but that at times had seemed so far away. I have incredible friends and family. I remain happily married, and I am the mom of twins, a boy and a girl. I get to travel the world and have a beautiful beachfront home, two helicopters, and a fighter jet. (Why not have a fighter jet? My husband is a stunt pilot.) I also love the work that I do and the people I work with, but what I value the most is that I get to do what I love professionally: work with great people and help others achieve success. But I can't help everyone, as much as I want to. There is only one thing that no one has figured out how to manufacture more of—time—and no cloning company that has pitched to me is close to being able to replicate humans, even if I wanted to try that. So I give as much as I can when I can to the people who call for advice every day—not just my employees and the people I invested in but people who read about me in the *New York Times* and other media, heard about my deals on the street, or worked with me in the past.

People who are striving to achieve, build, and scale their visions.

People who are stuck, scared or just baffled as to why they can't move forward.

People who are wondering why their ideas failed to gain traction while other people's similar ideas did.

"What should I do next, Kim?"

"How did you go from broke to millions?"

"Can you show me how to be successful?"

Good questions, and I've wanted to help answer them all. I'm an ordinary person, but I live an extraordinary life. How did I do it? I started taking notes.

What I Had Learned

Initially when I asked myself why I had succeeded, all I came up with were things that had not helped me.

I didn't grow up wealthy.

In school, I was an average student with average grades. It was my twin sister and older brother who were bused off to the gifted and talented school while I stayed back.

I didn't learn a special secret in college. I didn't graduate and say, "I will now execute at the highest level." I said what most kids said, "I want to make money." And ended up broke.

I ignored my parents' advice to find stability, control, and happiness.

I had always worked hard for everything I had as my parents expected, but hard work wasn't my point of difference. I worked hard at that dot-com, and I still failed. I know lots of people who work hard day after day and get nowhere.

It wasn't IQ either. How many intelligent people do you know who are still struggling to succeed or are toiling in obscurity in the companies they created or work for?

Maybe it was my sheer determination and will to succeed? I'm as ambitious and energetic as anyone I've met. I'm "go big or go home" in every aspect of my life. But does that make me different from tens of millions of other people?

I also didn't have one brilliant or unique idea. In fact, anyone can have a great idea. As an active angel investor, I get pitched dozens of ideas a week, and I have the opportunity to work with many successful individuals, entrepreneurs, and organizations to bring their visions to life. But ultimately, ideas are a dime a dozen, right?

And that's when it hit me:

Your idea is just a dream until you execute it.

Throughout my career, I've played many roles—founder, CEO, angel investor, wife, friend, mentor, mom—and the one skill that has driven my success more than anything else is:

Execution

Execution separates the dreamers from the doers: it is the ability to *do* and get results—to keep moving forward to achieve your vision and goals in business and life despite the challenges, hardships, and obstacles that lie ahead.

Execution is what I and the most successful entrepreneurs and leaders I have known had mastered. Execution disrupted complacency and markets. Regardless of role, organization, or industry, execution was the difference between success and failure.

As I explored this idea further, I found not only personal and anecdotal evidence for my belief but also supporting data. According to Harvard Business School professor Robert Kaplan and his colleague David Norton, 90 percent of business strategies *fail due to poor execution.*[1]

Furthermore, based on a *Harvard Business Review* database, employees at 60 percent of companies surveyed claimed that their organization was "weak" at execution.[2] Specifically, these respondents denied that their organizations were able to quickly translate important strategic and operational decisions into action.

What I believe is that those organizations failed to turn what they were doing into results and sustainable success. Action was only part of the equation. I had seen plenty of dreams get stuck in a nebulous place, whether they were caught in trying to begin the execution process or confused at how to continue once they began:

- Why did one person's vision or big idea never leave the garage or computer (or kitchen table) while similar ideas took off?

- Why did the most passionate people I know fail to translate their passion into success?
- Why can some people check-off everything on a to-do list and never move forward on their goals?
- Why did people resilient enough to pivot well in crises still fall short?
- Why can some people do all that but still find themselves alone—failing to work well with others or still struggling even if they did work well with others?

The answer is that those people didn't or couldn't execute.

Now here's the best news: execution is a skill that can be learned.

I know this because I learned it, and you can too. I didn't emerge from the womb a master at execution. That would be like saying I was born into leadership because I led my twin sister into the world by nine minutes. I don't believe I have an execution gene or that one even exists. My success didn't happen overnight either, and neither did the idea for this book. My method came way before my message. The successes I've achieved are the result and the proof that my methodology works.

And my message to you before you begin is this:

**You can change the course of your life
by mastering execution.**

Take the Execution Success Test!

If you haven't yet, now is the time to learn which one of the five traits you lead with—*vision, passion, action, resilience,* or *relationships*—by taking my five-minute free Execution Success Test at KimPerell.com.

Remember: Unlike other tests and quizzes that "label" people as one thing or another, you are not one type or another. This test will simply tell you the trait you lead with right now for perspective moving forward.

The Truth About Success

Growing up with two entrepreneurs for parents, I learned that success was almost never a straight line. Things rarely work out exactly as planned. They hit ditches. Encountered winding curves that left them headed in the wrong direction, forks in the road with no signs to tell them which way to go, and detours just when they thought they had finally reached their destination.

Flash forward to me as an adult on my own entrepreneurial journey. I was sitting in an airport, waiting to depart so I could get home to my family after another business trip, when I saw an image in my mind that looked something like Figure 1.1. I smiled at the accuracy of the image. Success only *looks* easy. It was the perfect summary of my parent's and my paths to success. A perfect summary of *everyone's path to success.* If I were more of an artist, I'd add a few dead ends in there. Some lows that dip under the bottom of the frame. A few of those forks I just mentioned.

Figure 1.1 **What Success Really Looks Like**

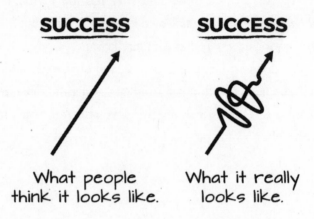

Success may appear easy, but it's never a straight line. It's an odyssey of sorts. This book will not change that. No book can. No *one* can.

While I can't straighten the line to success, I can show you how to prepare yourself for the pitfalls, setbacks, tough decisions, and hard work that will inevitably come. I can show you how to master the one skill that drives success (**execution**) and the five traits that propel great execution (the **execution factor**, Figure 1.2): vision, passion, action, resilience, and relationships.

Vision, passion, action, resilience, and **relationships:** These are the traits you need to develop into habits to execute at the highest level. But while I present the five traits of execution separately in this book, you will quickly learn that the execution factor is an ecosystem: interdependent, not independent. The traits are best viewed as equal parts of a circle with the point in the middle being execution at the highest level—the point where all five traits are deployed in balance. The point where I and every individual and company should strive to live every day.

Figure 1.2 **The Execution Factor**

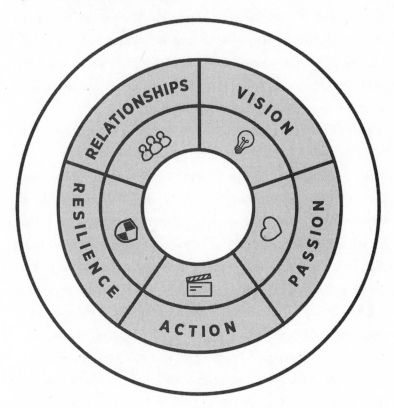

The Five Traits of the Execution Factor

The connective tissue of all the companies I have created, invested in, and worked for is that they all reached success by ensuring the five execution traits were represented in their leadership and people.

Vision: Your North Star

People who lead with Vision know where they're going. As the line to success weaves its messy way to the top, your vision is your compass, guiding you to your destination. Let me be clear: having a vision is not the same as being visionary. It's about having a clear picture of what you want to achieve. Without a clear vision, you don't know what goals to set or what actions to take. By taking charge of your vision, being exactingly clear about what you want, and following your North Star, you are setting yourself up for a life of greater success and fulfillment.

Just like running a marathon, your North Star can have a lot of checkpoints along the way. For example, my vision is to motivate and inspire others to achieve their dreams. Unfortunately, there's not enough time for me to meet with all the incredibly talented individuals with great ideas, so I am executing on my vision by writing this book, creating an execution platform, and using the proceeds to help fund as many individuals as possible. Just remember: No matter what your vision is, it's essential that you can see it and *feel* it. It must be meaningful to you so that you (and eventually others through you) genuinely connect to it. That connection is indispensable. It will make you more resilient, give you something to focus on when times get tough, and help you fight through the fear, uncertainty, and doubt.

Passion: What You're Willing to Sacrifice and Suffer For

How I see passion may be different from what you might assume or have read before. The word *passion* comes from Latin root *pati*, meaning suffering or enduring. Thus, *compassion* means "to suffer with" (the compassionate aren't immune to other people's pain). Think about all the times you have comforted a friend in pain or felt someone else's compassion. Passion is, at its core, a form of pain that demands it be quenched. Simply put, passion is not just about the things you *love* but about those things that you would happily *suffer* and *sacrifice* for. Therefore, mastering Passion in execution is about maintaining the emotional connection to your vision and goals. This level of emotion is necessary because it underpins almost everything good in our personal and professional lives: positivity, self-belief, learning, focus, satisfaction, and above all, motivation.

In the workplace, people who lead with passion often have relentless energy and determination that inspires commitment, engagement, and performance in others. Passion will give you and those around you a sense of meaning, sustain you through the seemingly unsustainable, and enable you to dig deep when it counts the most. Just remember: Our emotions drive the positive thoughts and feelings in our lives, but they also drive the negative ones!

Action: Taking That First Step and the Next One

People who lead with action know how to take the first step (arguably the most challenging) and then the next ones. They don't hesitate or get stuck in analysis paralysis. They know every time they act, they get one step closer to their goals. It's too easy to play it safe and wait for all the data. It's especially easy to get distracted when you're thinking far ahead. Leading with action doesn't mean discounting the importance of strategy and planning. Rather, it means knowing that all analyses and projections are only approximations and guesstimations. You don't know what will happen until you start, and action-oriented people know there is no wrong way to start.

People who lead with action seize the day to make things happen. They may be scared, and they feel the fear, but they push it aside and *do it anyway!* That's what I did when I got on that plane to Hawaii to start my first company. Was I scared? Yes, I was terrified I would fail. But I didn't let that stop me. I faced my fear and moved anyway. Just remember: Action without vision is just busyness, and it's important to not mistake busyness for progress. In a world of limited time and resources, you need to carefully choose where to invest your energy and not get stuck in a hamster wheel of repeating the same action over and over.

Resilience: Dealing with Obstacles, Change, and Uncertainty

People who lead with resilience accept uncertainty and overcome the inevitable obstacles and roadblocks to success. This allows them to thrive in change. There's an elasticity in their confidence. They bounce back after setbacks. They know how to handle a crisis, they have confidence and gumption in the face of impending doom, and throughout it all they demonstrate a tendency to recover stronger than before. They fail forward.

Resilience is not just about dealing with obstacles, crises, and setbacks. It's about dealing with them in constructive and creative ways. Resilient people know you can't change the wind but you can change your sail! This makes them inspiring—even stabilizing—influences when situations are intense, conditions are in chaos, or obstacles seem insurmountable. They believe *they have control* over the events in their lives even when the world seems to be working against them. They have heartset and mindset in balance so they know when to give up and when to continue despite the challenges that lie ahead.

Relationships: Having the Right People in Your Life

Building healthy, inspiring, supportive relationships is not just the cornerstone to successful execution. It's the cornerstone to happiness. The most significant element in any person's life is the people. We are biologically wired to connect with others, rely on those around us, and work together. In short, we are at our best when we have the capacity to collaborate. And of course, success is always better shared. Honestly, I wouldn't be where I am today without all the people who have helped and supported me along the way.

Great relationships aren't a luxury. They are a necessity. And like every other valuable asset, they need time, care, and attention in business just as in life. Those who know the power of relationships have an ability to recognize the strengths and talents of individuals and are guided by a win-win mentality, always on the lookout for areas of reciprocity and mutual success. They also know the importance of being with people who believe in them and provide the strength they need to transform their vision into reality. In fact, *if you change nothing else in your life than the people you spend your time with, you will have increased your chances of success tenfold.*

Ready, Set, Execute!

My life continues to be transformed by these five traits of execution, and I owe my success in business and life to mastering them. I use them all the time—whether planning our next family adventure, determining which entrepreneurs I want to invest in, working on the next big deal for my company, or writing this book.

Now you can master them too. *And if you think you have mastered them?* Know I work every day to execute better to achieve my life goals—and that means turning these traits into habits.

Mastering the five traits of execution will turn them into habits.

What does that mean? Habits are traits that have evolved into something settled and regular—something so ingrained that you do them almost without thinking about them. You want to make the five traits of execution habitual and simultaneously eliminate the bad habits that get in their way. Think of execution like exercise:

- If you stop working out parts of your body, it's not like working out the other parts will compensate. Eventually the parts you're not exercising will weaken.
- If you reach your goal working out, you can't stop exercising and magically maintain where you are. Eventually your body will start to decline.
- If you fail to work even harder to push past your goals once you reach them, it's unlikely you'll keep getting better and achieve new goals. You will just maintain how you are now.

For some people that may be fine. Not for me, however, and (I'm hoping) not for you. I want you to execute better in every aspect of your life and then *keep doing it better* so you don't just maintain but grow to achieve even more extraordinary things! In business, no one can afford to just "maintain" these days and hold off the competition—for your business or your job. All it takes for you to lose your job is one person or company who wants it more than you do and executes better.

Oh, and one more thing: *If you think these five traits sound simple?* You're right. And that's a *good* thing. This book and mastering execution is structured in a straightforward, concise way that gets results.

Remember: Simple and easy are two very different things—and people who think they know better often confuse the two. Besides, even when things are easy—and might save you some pain or even your life—people don't always do them. For example, who doesn't know putting on sunscreen prevents sunburn? Sunburns don't just hurt. Sun exposure is the leading cause of skin cancer, the most common cancer in the United States. *Yet according to the Centers for Disease Control and Prevention, fewer than two-thirds of all Americans wear sunscreen, even when they have nothing against it.*[3]

Truth is, it doesn't matter if you think these traits of execution are easy, simple, or challenging to execute, or somewhere in between. In reality, many people who fail to execute just aren't willing to take the time or won't commit themselves to do the work.

I didn't go from broke to multimillionaire. I went from broke to $100,000 and then from $100,000 to $1 million and then from $1 million to $10 million, and so on, recommitting myself to execute better after I reached each milestone. That's how I kept climbing. That's how I kept evolving. That's how I became the master of my success. Mastering execution will allow you to reach your goals and mark new milestones. To become an expert, it will take time and a willingness to get outside your comfort zone to hone your strengths *and* confront your weaknesses. The people and companies I know who have mastered execution understand they need all five traits to be successful. It's a balance.

Think back to earlier in this chapter to my list of questions about why people fail to execute. Remember those people who check off everything on their to-do lists but never move forward and deliver results on their goals? They've often lost touch with their vision and stop making progress because action without vision is just busyness. But vision without action is just dreaming. Passion without resilience will leave you unable to bounce back from setbacks. Resilience without vision can leave you course correcting to oblivion. If you use all the traits but you don't have the right relationships and you don't actually value the people in your life, you won't get to where you need and want to be—because no one is successful alone.

This is why you can't just focus on the trait you lead with. It's like building an arch: the structure can be strong and complete only when all the traits are working in tandem. You need to develop *all* the traits to navigate the ups and downs and the zigs and zags of success. If you took the Execution Success Test, you know which trait that is. However, you must remember this: the trait you lead with—and any trait you master—can be a great advantage and disadvantage as you execute. It's a double-edged sword. Sometimes, you *can* have too much of a good thing, and when you do, that's when the traits on the opposite side of the circle get ignored. For example, when I am deep in Action and ready to *do do do*, I have to make sure I am still considering the needs of others, not steamrolling other good ideas, or having my people do only what they are told and nothing else. The reverse is also true. If I spend too much time analyzing the pros and cons of an opportunity, I might never *act*.

Think of the traits of execution as being like the forces of nature around us. The sun is vision, the water is passion, fire is action, earth is resilience, and the winds are relationships—*beautiful, harmonious, and powerful in balance but potentially dangerous in extremes.*

Finally, before we continue, please know that *none of what you read and do when it comes to execution will lead to success if what you are doing isn't personally meaningful.*

Throughout this book, I want you to be thinking about how this material specifically relates to *you*. To make sure, I'll be giving you Pulse Check exercises as you read, and at the end of every chapter I'll be giving you self-reflection activities and questions.

Those reflections start now.

What do you hope to get out of this book?

Something brought you to this point. What is it? An idea you want to bring to reality? A business you want to get started? A promotion you want to achieve? A boss asking you to step up? Perhaps you've just experienced a major failure or disappointment, and you want to have the skills to handle it better next time.

All that and more is possible, but there is also a bigger, more important question you must answer too:

*Why are **you** here?*

Not just what do you hope to achieve, but *why*. If you don't know where you're going, how do you expect to get there? Movement in many directions is not progress. It's chaos. Splintered attention to a goal can bring you more pain than relief, but you can have different actions supporting your vision. You can even have different visions—personal and professional—at the same time. But you have to know what they are and why they are important to you to truly commit.

So . . . *why are **you** here?*

Take a moment to answer and write your answer down before continuing. You've got this!

VISION

Your North Star

*Don't let small minds convince you
your dreams are too big.*
—ANONYMOUS

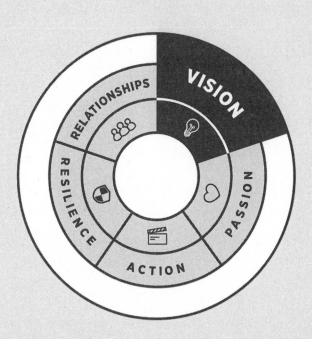

2

Moon Shot

May 1961. The height of the Cold War. The previous month had been brutal for the United States. The Berlin Wall had gone up. The CIA-trained force leading the Bay of Pigs Invasion in Cuba to unseat Castro was unsuccessful. And NASA's space program was failing as the Soviet Union's cosmonaut Yuri Gagarin became the first human to reach space and orbit the Earth.

President John F. Kennedy knew America needed a vision—something that would rally the nation, inflate its heart, and inspire dreams. He delivered. By the end of the decade, he told a joint session of Congress, our nation would put a man on the moon and return him safely to Earth.

Less than a year later, in February 1962, John Glenn became the first American to orbit the Earth, and NASA was back in the game. Kennedy renewed his commitment to his vision with these riveting words: "We choose to go to the moon in this decade and do the other things, not because they are easy, but because they are hard, because that goal will serve to organize and measure the best of our energies and skills, because that challenge is one that we are willing to accept, one we are unwilling to postpone, and one which we intend to win, and the others, too."[1]

On July 20, 1969, more than five years after Kennedy's assassination, the *Eagle* landed, and American Neil Armstrong became the first man to step on the moon. Our nation would need all the traits of execution to get there, but it was Kennedy's vision that kept the country motivated and drove us through it all.

As an entrepreneur, I have always shot for the moon and found inspiration for my vision by following what I call my North Star.

Your North Star

I have always had a North Star in my life: one big and bright vision that the rest of my life revolves around—an inner compass that fuels my passion and determines my actions. When my vision is clear and compelling, I know where I am and where I'm going. This is an empowered state that has served me well, and it also happens to be the starting point for the first trait to master to execute at the highest levels: vision.

Having a vision is not the same as being a visionary. It's not about seeing five moves ahead or building a better mousetrap. Those are things you do to achieve your vision. A vision is about having a crystal-clear picture of something you want to achieve, as Kennedy did. The most successful people I know have a clear vision of what they want to achieve—a North Star to maintain their focus in a world of distractions.

Those who don't have a vision are like Alice, lost in Wonderland, asking the Cheshire Cat, "Would you tell me, please, which way I ought to go from here?"

The Cat asks where she wants to get to.

"I don't much care where," says Alice.

"Then it doesn't matter which way you go," says the Cat.

Those Who Lead with Vision
Know Where They're Going

Where do you want to go? What's your vision for your life? Are you Alice or the Cat? I've always had a vision of the life I wanted to live. I wanted to run stuff. I wanted to make things happen. When I was a kid, I saw my parents get knocked down and get back up to keep pursuing their vision of a great life for us. My childhood vision of that great life was more about immediate gratification—earning money to get the things I wanted: an ice cream, horseback riding lessons, a car. By the time I graduated from college, broke and in debt to my parents, my vision had evolved. I wanted to earn my financial freedom. I had considered those traditional jobs in investment banking and marketing, but I knew, with the vision I had, I needed to do something different. I needed to find a job that had high opportunity, and that meant high risk. So I took the job at the Internet startup before the dot-com bubble burst.

You know how that turned out: the company went bankrupt, and I found myself broke again at 23. I was devastated. However, that experience helped me change direction on how I was going to achieve my vision of living an incredible life: I needed to create it myself. I didn't just want to live an incredible life with financial freedom. I wanted to be in charge of my own destiny. I fought through my fear—and the voices around me and in my head that told me to take a more stable career path—and started my own company.

Again, you know how that turned out: my first company thrived, and I sold it for $30 million. The company had grown to over $100 million in revenue, and I had achieved my vision for that great life. But that success, first and foremost, had nothing to do with what business I was in or the tactics I took. I certainly never had a vision to build and run a digital marketing company selling remote control toys, teeth whiteners, and wrinkle reducers. I did have the vision for freedom and control of my life, and I did everything it took to get there.

My vision wasn't to build a company and sell it. My vision was to maintain the extraordinary life I had built. On the beach. With my husband. Start a family. No matter what was thrown at me or what challenge was looming on the horizon, I never lost sight of that North Star. It guided me to where I am today. By focusing on it relentlessly, my chances of success increased exponentially. Sure I had other visions—call them *sub-visions* or *micro-visions*—going at any time, but I've found that it's important to have one that is front and center, a pilot commanding my focus and energy. Visions can also grow and change and evolve. The point is that at any time, you have that clear vision. Then you can look at what goals you'd like to set or actions you need to take to get there. Your vision gives those actions purpose and meaning. The work is hard, but your vision drives you forward.

Without a clear vision you can see *and feel*, you don't know what goals to set or what actions to take.

By taking charge of your vision, being crystal clear about what you want, and staying on track with your North Star, you are setting yourself up for a life of greater success and fulfillment. Maybe you know this already. Maybe you're like me and have a clear picture of your life vision, and that's your driving force. Or maybe your vision right now is about a dream, a big goal you'd like to accomplish, or something you'd like to do. Doesn't matter if it is all, some, or none of these.

Mastering the skill of execution starts by articulating and understanding what your vision is. Vision is first and foremost your guide to where you are going and what you will do with your life, not what you are doing presently:

- You can have a vision about the major purpose of your life (such as making a positive impact on people or the environment or having financial freedom).
- You can have a vision of what you want to do (like being an artist or a learning to cook).
- You can have a vision that's a dream you'd like to become reality (like buying a house or starting a new business).
- You can have a vision that's a big goal (like running a marathon or traveling the world).

The list above by no means covers the spectrum of what your vision can be. The most important thing is that you have one. **No matter what it is, you must be able to see it and *feel* it clearly.** So without further ado, let's look at your vision.

Vision Pulse Check

What vision is driving you right now? Write it down. Don't worry if you're not quite sure. I know we are jumping right into this, so if you're feeling really stuck, think about what brought you to this book. I'm guessing there is something you want to do, build, create, accomplish, or make happen. What is it?

How did that go for you? Did you see and feel your vision? Was it crystal clear and right out in front of you?

Don't worry if the exercise was difficult: Your vision needs to be uncomplicated, but the process of articulating your vision, let alone executing it, is often far from easy. And don't worry if your vision doesn't feel exactly right. Whether you are dreaming big or starting small, you'll have a chance to review, refine, or maybe even change it as we move forward, so it doesn't have to be perfect right now. This is just the first step to finding your North Star—that inner compass. The next steps involve defining and refining your North Star no matter how clear you think it is already and building guardrails so you won't get lost in your vision as you try to achieve it.

Questions for Self-Reflection

Before continuing, look again at your vision:

> Do you feel that this vision is clear, compelling, and meaningful to you?

> Do you feel comfortable that this is the right vision for you—even if you're not sure how you're going to get there?

> Can you easily articulate your North Star to others in one sentence?

If the answer to any of these questions is no, please go back and revise your vision.

3

Living Someone Else's Dream

According to friends and family and a few people at work, Darren made "the best chili in the entire world." They begged him to make it and to bring it to parties and potlucks. Every time he did, they exclaimed, "This is so good! You should open a food truck! You'd make millions."

For his part, Darren never dreamed about owning a food truck—or a restaurant or anything else in the food business. He was a maintenance manager for a hospital. Had been for 17 years. He had nothing to do with food service. But every time he made the chili, he heard the same thing: "We can totally see you doing it." There was just one problem: Darren didn't. Eventually he started wondering if he should . . .

Owning a food truck didn't seem like much fun when Darren thought about it. He didn't even eat at them much, preferring to bring his lunch to work to save money. Some quick searches on Google indicated the business was tough—as tough as the restaurant business, which has a very high failure rate. But food trucks were making up a growing scene around town. When he took his lunch outside, he always saw lines at the half dozen or so that parked on the street near the hospital. He watched the people working the trucks and he talked to the owners. They all loved what they were doing.

Darren didn't think he would love it, but how could so many people he loved be wrong? He started seeing dollar signs and pushed himself to make it happen.

After the kids were asleep, he worked on the truck. He invested his savings. He created a business plan, but the bank didn't see his vision, and he got turned down for a small business loan. Instead, he borrowed some funds from his parents and a few of those friends who had been egging him on. When he needed more time to make it work, he chalked up his lack of progress to his day job, and he quit to devote himself full time. He took classes on food safety and prep in order to get his license.

After one of the owners of another food truck around town invited him to work a shift with her, Darren accepted, and the next day he brought her some of his chili.

"It's delicious," she said, and then she noted how unhappy he looked all day. "Did you have fun yesterday?"

Darren nodded his head yes, but he knew he didn't mean it, and she didn't buy it either. To her, Darren just seemed stressed and angry. "Are you sure you want to do this?" she asked.

"I will . . . eventually," Darren said.

He *wanted* to believe that—wanted to believe he would eventually want to do this and be able to have the vision of himself in his truck, serving chili to long lines, having fun. Other people saw that for him, but he doubted more and more every day that he ever would. A few weeks later, still stressed and now angry all the time, Darren was broke. He sold the truck, paid back what he could, and thankfully was able to get a job doing the work he loved: maintenance.

What happened? Why did Darren fail to execute on his vision and succeed—or even see the vision come to life? Because he never wanted to open a food truck. Making chili for friends and family that made them happy was what he liked to do. He could be on his feet all day chopping, stirring, and cleaning to serve chili to everyone he loved, but he had no desire to do those things to serve strangers. The food truck was *their vision for him.*

Refining Your Vision

When Darren listened to his dreams of dollars and what others envisioned for him rather than what he saw for himself, he violated all three of the three critical elements for refining your vision to ensure that you have all the necessary components to bring it life. No matter your vision, big or small, the desire to make money is not enough to do that.

Your vision must

- Be crystal clear.
- Be meaningful.
- Feel comfortable and congruent with who you are.

Be Crystal Clear

You need to be able to see your vision, feel it, and touch it. You must then be able to clearly articulate that vision to yourself and others.

Darren never saw his vision for his food truck; only others did. That won't work. People without passion are transparent. People see right through you, sometimes before you do, like the bank that rejected Darren's loan and the woman who owned the food truck.

As I said, I have always had a crystal-clear vision of my life and the life I wanted to live. As a kid, I could see working for what I wanted, working for my financial independence after college, and controlling my own destiny and being accountable for my own day-to-day actions when I started my own company. That clarity is one of the tenets of my success. I had to make sure my vision was crystal clear to those who worked with and for me. They may have had their own visions to pursue, but I needed them to share and help me achieve mine. They needed to be crystal clear on that in order to truly believe in the importance of where we were going. They had to see my purpose—know my "why." People work for people, not companies. A connection to your vision only reaffirms that paradigm. The legendary Sam Walton was famous for knowing every janitor by name at his Walmart stores when he shook their hands—and they wanted to shake his. It was crystal clear that they were on their journeys together.

Be Meaningful

Your vision must be something you feel connected to from the beginning. It must compel your passion. Thus, it's essential to ask yourself, "Why is this vision important to me?"

Darren loved his friends and cooking chili for them. Where he went off the rails was trying to extend that vision to something that wasn't meaningful to him and expecting that he eventually would come around. Does that mean if the food truck had been meaningful to Darren or if he had been passionate about food trucks, he would have succeeded? Of course not. But even success would have been meaningless to him, which might have been a fate sadder than failure.

Unlike Darren, I liked what I did and enjoyed the process, but what made it meaningful was my vision for living an extraordinary life. It was a constant reminder of what I was in it for and why I had to stay committed. The only way I could see getting that was to go out on my own and feel the freedom that doing so gave me to do the things I wanted. I could go to the gym at noon and work until 2 a.m. See a midday matinee or sit and just listen to the ocean waves. What allowed me to revel in my freedom was that I never wavered from my vision. That kept me focused and fostered my passion. When I brought others on board, they never doubted how much this meant to me, and I learned to let it foster their passion too.

Feel Comfortable and Congruent with Who You Are
Your vision must be exactly that: yours.

I admired Darren's willingness to go all in, and he definitely loved cooking and making chili. But that wasn't enough. He never ate at food trucks or worked in the food industry. It would have been far cheaper to test the waters by working a shift at a truck before he was blinded by dollar signs and bought his own truck. He had never charged anyone for food or cooked for complete strangers. He could have entered something like a chili cook-off, seen how it felt to cook for people he didn't know, and have them judge him. Then he might have known if the food truck dream was his or someone else's. After all, just because you're good at something doesn't necessarily mean that it is a passion of yours. Sometimes we like to just enjoy the skills for what they are rather than developing or monetizing them—like a musical instrument you enjoyed messing around with but never wanted to take lessons on.

You must instinctively feel comfortable with your vision. There should be no reservations. If you have them, you need to investigate that uncertainty. If you have a sense of anger, stress, or doubt when you think about your vision, take some time to assess why. Double-check that it's what is right for you and what you truly want. I'm not talking about fear or anxiety and whether you can be successful. Those feelings are normal. As I said, when I started my own company, I was terrified. But I *knew* my vision was right. In fact, it was *who I am*. As a child of entrepreneurs, this vision of freedom was in my bones. This gave me an acute ability to identify when I was chasing a dream for me, not being pressured to chase one that wasn't mine. Too often our visions are something others want or expect from us, and that creates a distance from what we truly desire. My parents let me figure this out for myself, and you must as well.

Bringing Your Vision to Life

Now that you know the three essential components for refining your vision, I'm going to tell you a story about seeing your vision and bringing it to life. It's personal to me, a family heirloom that's been passed down for generations. My grandfather told it to my dad, who told it to me and my sister when we were kids, and it is a great illustration of this idea.

Two young men were working on the railroad, laying track beside each other every single day for a year. They had lunch every day and talked about everything from their families to current events to music to what would come next after this part of the job was finished. When the job was done, the men were sent to new jobs far from each other. They fell out of touch.

In his new location, one man befriended the foreman, and he asked the foreman about learning new skills and how the company worked. He eventually became the foreman of his own crew, and he worked his way up over 30 years to become a regional president of the railroad itself, overseeing its ever-expanding operations. On one of his tours of the rails, the president saw a familiar face among the tracklayers about to have lunch. The face was older and more weathered than the one he knew, but he recognized it instantly.

The president disembarked from his railcar office and approached the man. "I know you," he said. "We used to work together on these railroads."

The two men exchanged a warm handshake and a laugh, and the president invited the man into his railcar to have lunch for an hour in honor of the hundreds of hours they had shared decades ago. They spent the time catching up and reminiscing about the old days. But there was a sting of sadness for one of the men because the "old days" were his current ones. Before they parted, the president asked the other man why he had never tried to work his way up the ranks the way he had. His friend responded, "I get paid to lay track."

That was the fundamental difference between the president and the tracklayer: one went to work for a paycheck; the other went to work for the railroad. One was building the company; the other was building the track.

As I grew up, I carried this story and its lesson close to my heart. My grandfather was one of the biggest influences on my business mind. My dad was a serial entrepreneur, but my grandfather was a prominent turnaround CEO, and he had a special kind of vision. He would go into a troubled company, see what it needed, and devote his passion to fixing it up. He tirelessly fought through the obstacles to turn it around, built relationships inside and out to get it sold, and then promptly got fired by the new owners. He then started all over again with a new company.

My grandfather was the execution factor incarnate. He was so good at it that the *Wall Street Journal* profiled his career in 1972. What's more impressive is that my grandfather worked himself up from the coal mines to get his education before he had the vision to become the savior of those companies.

Given his history, I thought the railroad story was true.

It wasn't.

I found that out later in life when I heard similar stories. I'm sure you've heard similar ones too. Sometimes the men are construction workers or fishermen. I've heard it told in parable form in which a man comes across two bricklayers at a building site and asks them what they are doing. One says he is laying bricks; the other says he is building a cathedral. My personal favorite (and one that is appropriate for how this chapter started) is the one in which President Kennedy visits NASA and comes across a young man sweeping the floors. He asks the man if he likes sweeping the floors at NASA, and the man says, "I'm not sweeping floors. I'm helping send a man to the moon."

The fact that none of these stories are true does not diminish their power to me. In fact, they only reinforce the point of how much more engaged and committed people are who see the railroad beyond the track, the cathedral beyond the bricks, and the moon beyond the broom.

. . . .

Painting a crystal-clear picture of what you
want to achieve and knowing exactly what it
will look like when you get there is essential.

. . . .

Visions will help clarify and keep you focused on what's important to you. They can also express your meaning and purpose. The equation is simple: the vision you have determines your commitment and the meaning of what you are doing. All you need to do is bring your vision to life. Michelangelo believed that all his sculptures were alive inside the block of marble, and it was his job to carve them out and let them breathe. Your first step is not to start sculpting yet but to use the process of visualization—to see beyond the possibilities that are right in front of you.

Imagery is incredibly powerful in directing our conscious and even unconscious behaviors. Images penetrate the entire mind and influence us in more ways than we can see. A lot of research supports how visualizing an action or an outcome makes you much more likely to be able to execute it. Sometimes it leads to success even without action. In one study, subjects were divided into two groups. For one month one group did conditioning exercises on their arms; the other simply visualized doing the exercises. At the end of the month, those who exercised their biceps increased muscle mass by 28 percent.

What's fascinating is that those who merely imagined doing the exercise increased muscle mass by 24 percent! Those who simply **visualized** the exercises physically saw changes. Wild, right?[1]

This is why visualization as a practice is so important: every time you see yourself doing an action, you are actually using the same neural pathways that you use to actually perform that action. Therefore, repetitive visualization will reinforce the message as well as the action. If you get specific and clear about what you want and you are able to see it—to animate and really picture it—then you can make it happen. That's because seeing is more than believing. A vision elicits emotion. It can fire you up, clarify your goals, and help you stay focused. Your body, mind, and spirit can devote themselves to something you can see. Think about all the powerful words that have *sight* in them that represent wisdom: *insight, foresight, hindsight,* and others.

One great way to do this is to visualize your vision as if you have already achieved it, to give yourself a bird's-eye view of your achievement. Imagine yourself being successful. What would you see, hear, or feel if you had achieved the vision already? Really put yourself in the feeling as if it has already happened. For example, if your vision is to start your own business, how can you bring that vision to life?

- What would you **see**? Is it a small office or a big building? Are you working on your own or with a team? What does it look like? Can you picture running meetings in a conference room?
- What would you **feel**? Is it the excitement of sitting at your desk each morning, or pitching your business to potential investors? What would the energy be like?
- What would you **hear**? Is it the buzz of staff or the ring of a bell with each sale? Is it the interview where someone is asking how you got there?

It's important to note that none of these questions have anything to do with what you might call "goal setting." You can't break down a vision into goals and actionable steps if you can't see it in your mind. How can you know what it will take to achieve a vision if you haven't mapped the steps to get there and you don't know what you are looking for? Right now is the time to make sure that what you see is as big as it can be. Whether your vision is big or small, make sure it is the railroad, cathedral, or moon of its kind!

The biggest mistake you can ever make is not to dream big, expansive, or bold enough. Experience and data may tell you otherwise, but they are only two of the many factors that go into your vision. Yes, your vision must be real, not a mirage or a hallucination. This isn't about wishful thinking. Your vision needs to be based on reality, but it needs to include the biggest opportunities and possibilities you can see. But beware! There is one area where vision building can get you into trouble: if you see a vision that has little basis in *your* reality.

. . . .

**Whatever your dream is,
dream it bigger and start now.**

. . . .

People may treat them as synonyms, but *reality* and *realistic* are two different things. I'm grounded in reality, but like Kennedy's moon shot vision, I never believe that anything I can visualize is unrealistic. That's self-limiting. Which is why I never hesitated to get on that plane to Hawaii with just a laptop, a $10,000 loan, and the experience and relationships I had to start my first company.

I admit that even I sold my vision short. I never saw my first company growing beyond $50 million in revenue or ever reaching $100 million. But after selling my vision short, I never let it happen again—and I don't want it to happen to you. It's critical that your belief in yourself is stronger anyone else's doubt.

How big you see yourself growing is part of your North Star burning at its brightest. Trust me, you are ablaze with opportunity.

VISION CHECK

Questions for Self-Reflection

Reflect on the vision that you wrote out in the last chapter, and take a few moments to answer the questions below to make sure your vision is exactly what it needs to be. Close your eyes and visualize it as if you had already achieved your vision:

What do you see?

What do you hear?

What do you feel?

Remember: Specificity will help you bring it to life.

4

Don't Just Think It, Ink It

O n June 10, 2014, the headline plastered across the *TechCrunch* home page read:

BAM! Amobee Buys Adconion for $235 Million

But unlike the sale of my first company in 2008 to Adconion, I knew this sale was going to happen. In fact, this headline *was* my vision. I had visualized it in my mind almost a year before and then seen it every day since. I had written down my goal to sell to Singtel (Amobee's parent company), a date, and a publication on a piece of notepaper and taped it to my bathroom mirror. I had looked at my dream and myself every day.

My vision propelled me forward in the months it took close the deal. It kept me motivated as I worked to get meetings with the mergers and acquisitions team at Amobee. It didn't let me get discouraged when the banker I hired had to wait months to do his job because when I brought him on, we weren't as close to closing the sale as I thought we were. We were going to get there! It helped me keep hope alive and energized when I started to wonder if I could pull it off. Even when the doubt inevitably trickled in during the year before closing, I returned to my vision on the mirror—my windshield wiper clearing the view ahead. Through the setbacks, obstacles, and enormous amount of time and energy it took, I never gave up. I persevered.

I really don't think I could have done it if I hadn't been able to see that vision on my mirror every morning and night I was home. If I hadn't kept a relentless focus and energy at closing this deal, I would have floundered. But my North Star was on that piece of paper, and it guided me for nearly a year, as I lived to turn my vision into reality.

There are distractions at every corner, deadlines, meetings, relationships to maintain, fires to put out, employees who need your time, family and friends who need you—how do you stay on track and faithful to your vision? With the world swirling around you, how can you make sure you're mindful of distractions and other events that threaten to take you off course?

Two ways:

1. Write your vision down where you can see it daily.
2. Use that as a reminder of how to prioritize your time daily.

It's that simple! These two points will have a huge impact on your ability to stay on track with your goal to execute your vision successfully.

Write Your Vision Down and
Review It Regularly

The importance of having goals has been well documented for decades. Research by Edwin Locke, one of the pioneers in researching goal setting and its impact on performance, found that having specific and challenging goals led to a much higher performance than did having easy or no goals.[1]

But just having goals is not enough. You need to write that vision down. That way, it reinforces what you have brought to life in your mind, compels you to think about it every day, and makes you articulate and focus on it and share it with the world (or at least anyone who shares your bathroom).

Vision Pulse Check

Right now, find a place to write your vision down where you can see and review it regularly. Maybe it's on your laptop. Maybe it's in a notebook or planner. Maybe it's on *your* bathroom mirror!

If you don't write it down, it will soon be out of sight and out of mind.

According to research by David Kohl, professor emeritus at Virginia Tech, 80 percent of Americans do not have any type of definable goals. In fact, Professor Kohl reports that of the 20 percent who have goals, 16 percent don't write them down and

3 percent write them down but don't review them. That means only 1 percent of people have goals, write them down, *and* review them on a regular basis.[2] *Only 1 percent!?* That's a 1 percent everyone should want to be a part of no matter what they believe in. These are the people who are most successful for an action everyone has in their power to achieve but precious few do.

Kohl also suggests that people who write down their goals earn nine times as much over their lifetime as people who don't have goals. So don't just think it. Ink it!

Prioritize Your Vision

"The key is not to prioritize what's on your schedule, but to schedule your priorities." I love that Stephen Covey line. He wrote it decades ago, back when a tweet was just a bird noise.

Today, distraction is everywhere, starting with the phones in our hands. According to Steelcase, the typical office worker gets interrupted every 11 minutes and receives more than 100 e-mails a day. It's easy for your vision to get lost in the sea of texts and to-do lists. There's nothing wrong with those lists, but you *must* keep pushing your vision back to the top of any list you make, especially when more urgent—but not necessarily more important—items start to take up too much space.

Your vision should always be a priority.
You need to make time to execute your vision.

Scheduling your priorities for your vision and then reprioritizing them every day means you are focused on the action steps
that are required from you to execute. This includes minimizing the noise in your life and increasing your bandwidth to la-
ser focus on what's most important to achieving your vision. I
consciously built a support system around me that allows me
to concentrate on my strengths. I don't waste mental energy on
things I don't believe will absolutely contribute in some way to
achieving my vision. My friends tease me that I am the least ed-
ucated person they know on pop culture—songs, TV shows, ce-
lebrities, podcasts, fashion . . . the list goes on. But I'm happy to
sacrifice knowing what's trendy in order to prioritize my vision.

In addition to my bathroom mirror, I have my vision on the
notepad of my computer, where I keep all my to-dos. Every time I
open the notepad, there it is, reinforcing the actions I need to take
and making sure I don't lose sight of my North Star. Crossing off
things on a to-do list means nothing if those things are not directly related in some way to your North Star. If they aren't, you
need to think about why and if the things you are doing matter:

- Whenever there is a possibility of change, determine what
  impact that will have on your vision. Will it take you closer
  or further away from your vision? Perhaps there is something you should not be or don't need to be doing and need
  to hand over to someone else. Perhaps there is something
  you think you should be doing, but it doesn't matter as
  much as you think. Perhaps the things you are doing pla-
  cate the people yelling the loudest for attention. Perhaps
  you are focusing too much on others before yourself.

- Make a point to regularly review your actions specifically as they relate to your vision. We'll get into this on a
  deeper level in Trait 3, "Action." For now, one way to prioritize your vision is simply to give time to it. Ask yourself, "What time am I committing to my vision each day
  or at least weekly?"

If your vision is directly related to your day job, those two
things should be easy. Shut the door, walk to a quiet room, put
caution tape around your cubicle . . . whatever it takes to make
the time. For other types of visions, you're going to need to carve
out time. This means you will need to spend *less* time somewhere
else and stop doing something that isn't serving you. For me, I
stopped watching TV. Sure, I find time for the occasional show,
but I don't watch TV as much as I used to.

*What are you going to stop doing so you can give more time
to **your** vision?*

In the end, think of your vision as the story you want to write
for yourself and share with the world. Think of it like your favorite story as a kid. Personally, I loved *Where the Wild Things Are*.
Did you know Maurice Sendak wrote the book based on his vision of his childhood experiences? He was often in bed and sent
there without any supper. The wild things he encounters in the
jungle his room becomes were based on his family, and they are
menacing until Max intimidates them all and becomes their king.
But Max soon realizes he feels lonely and misses his family. He
decides to return home to the people he loves instead of getting
more lost in the vision he created.

These are perfect words of warning to all people who lead and get lost in vision when trying to execute: visions are nothing but dreams without action.

VISION CHECK
Questions for Self-Reflection

What could get in the way, or pull you off track of achieving the vision you wrote down?

How are you going to give and plan more time to your vision? What are you going to stop doing so you have more time to it?

How will you know if you're off track and out of alignment with your vision?

5

The Loneliest Trait

My parents met in Youngstown, Ohio, but they had no desire to settle there. They had a vision of their future and after college set off to find it. Since this was long before the Internet and because pictures in guidebooks could only say so much, they took three months to drive around the United States—down to the South, through Texas, across the Mountain West and the desert. Wherever they ended up, they'd camp and backpack, doing pretty much whatever they wanted as long as it stayed under their budget of $20 a day.

New Mexico seemed nice, but the heat was stifling. San Diego had perfect weather, but my dad wasn't crazy about its suburban sprawl. They finally settled on Portland, Oregon, with its mix of urban opportunity and outdoor life, the mountains and the ocean just an hour away. Ironically, what also attracted my parents to Portland was the notion that the city would keep them away from entrepreneurialism. It didn't.

Since my mom took time off to raise me, my twin sister, and my older brother, my father became my first role model for what an entrepreneur could be. Both of my parents are passionate, driven, giving people, but my dad inspired me to go after the biggest vision I have in life and never let up until I achieve it. The man was, and still is, tireless—relentless. He's a real shoot-the-moon type. While my mother was practical and pragmatic, Dad had the boundless confidence and unwavering determination to explore over-the-top ideas. What does the world need? What can I contribute? How can I create that?

While Dad hired people to do various tasks, he often took care of everything. When he was in property development, he was out there building and figuring out ways to modernize the work. It's no wonder I loved going to work with him and spending my weekends at his construction sites. Most of my life, my dad would be gone for a few days every week pursuing whatever boundless vision he had for the future and where the opportunities were: a self-service auto repair garage, roofing tiles, real estate, restaurants, bars, and beyond. As I write this book, he has turned 70, and is developing a residential care business that he believes will transform healthcare services for the elderly.

My dad will never retire. He can't. Like many people who lead with vision, Dad needs to keep exploring, building, and pushing forward to bring his vision to life. People like my dad love to create—and they keep finding new ideas to work on any hour of the day. If I call my dad on my way home at 8 p.m. after more than 12 hours at work, he'll never fail to ask why I am "taking off so early." Only part of him is joking because my dad always believes he can be doing more in business.

When People Get Stuck in a Vision

But while my dad is my inspiration, he is also my first cautionary tale for what happens when people get stuck in vision—and what happens when they get bored with the visions they have and lose focus.

Dad's forte is not maintaining what he builds or operationalizing it. As a result, people like my dad fail to execute at the level they could or should. Their drive gets them into risky deals and high-stakes investments, and they are blinded by what they believe is possible. They can also commit to something so risky it endangers not just the businesses but also their families, and sometimes they lose it all.

That's the ultimate pitfall for people stuck in vision: they can't let go no matter what the consequences are.

The best way to describe how my dad and I are different is how we gamble when we go to Las Vegas. When I win, I take some money off the table and hold on to it and let the rest ride. I take chances, but I am very careful to calculate the bets I am willing to make. My dad will never take money off the table. He will go all in with all he has. He doesn't care if he loses it all as long as he has a chance to make it big. That's his attitude: "Let's just go for it, make our luck, and seize the possibilities to change the world."

Five Tips for Not Getting Lost in Vision

There are many wonderful things about my father that I try to emulate every day. But how can you be the best parts of my dad and other visionaries and not get lost in the trappings of your vision? How can you avoid letting your vision consume you so much that it affects and even corrupts all other parts of execution?

1. Don't get lost in thinking.
2. Understand timing is everything.
3. Know ideas are a dime a dozen.
4. Make sure your vision is a business.
5. Accept that feedback is a gift.

1. Don't Get Lost in Thinking

The vision space can be exciting and energizing, but be careful you don't spend too much time thinking and not enough time doing. My dad was *always* thinking about what comes next. As a result, he would lose focus on one vision while he started to envision something else.

This overlap can be mistaken for progress. He's a warning for people who are stuck within the same vision while trying to grow it. You agonize so much about what's next that you don't act enough or take the right action to execute and operationalize the vision you're on. That's drive without direction.

2. Understand Timing Is Everything

My dad's first business—a self-serve auto shop—sounded great (even cool), but in the end, there was no market for it. Many people get stuck in vision because they forget to research if a market is there and to establish checkpoints to know if what they're doing is working. In my dad's auto shop case, it wasn't working. If no one is buying what you're selling, even if you're doing everything right, then there just isn't a market—yet or at all. Yes, your vision could be ahead of its time, but that does not mean you can will a market into existence and then execute.

The first company I worked for tried to sell cloud storage more than a decade before the infrastructure and demand could support its cost—and we burned through all our money trying to execute that vision. Like so many too-early visions, we ran out of money before our time.

3. Know Ideas Are a Dime a Dozen

This book is not about quitting your job because you have a great idea. Everyone has a great idea. I always say ideas are a dime a dozen. It's all about *executing* your idea. So many people fail to see that about their visions. To them, their visions are so crystal clear and real, they think everyone knows what it will take to execute them.

See why this is lofty? The visions are so alive in their heads—so tangible to them—that they proclaim it will take no time to execute them. As a result, they lack the patience to explain their vision to anyone more than once, let alone with any depth. *"The steps are so obvious and easy! We just need to build a platform for people to do X and then Y, and then Z will happen!"* No, they won't. You need to understand and be crystal clear about the value around what comes next.

4. Make Sure Your Vision Is a Business

People who lead with vision can get so caught up in their ideas that they not only fail to see the work it will take to execute them but they also fail to develop the commercial business sense to take their ideas to the next level. They may learn how to produce what they're selling, but have no idea how to make money on it. Hint: If you are losing money on every sale, you are not going to make money simply by selling more—no matter how well you execute. You might make millions, but you will burn through much more.

For aspiring entrepreneurs, I recommend not quitting your day job immediately to chase your vision. It's necessary to get some experience working on your venture while having the safety net of a job. Start preparing. Create some savings. Lower your expenses, and work on getting your contingency plan in place. Proactively and purposefully dedicate your off-work hours to your new venture to determine the viability of your new business. Get affirmation. You shouldn't leave your day job until you know you can meet your key monetary needs. (Note that this can be a savings plan—perhaps you have six months of living expenses you can use to fund your new venture.)

Think about all those people on the TV show *Shark Tank* who think that they just need an investment from the sharks to keep doing what they are doing with a losing operation—and they want to keep control. Even if the sharks believe in what is being pitched, they know the person in the tank is the wrong one to invest in. They will never execute on the highest levels if they refuse to listen and develop some business acumen.

5. Accept That Feedback Is a Gift

It's important to ask for constructive feedback to identify the blind spots and potential roadblocks that may get in your way—especially from people who don't think or act the way you do. Because if everyone sees or acts the same way as you do with your vision, you'll just be stuck together in the same car. You'll sit around and talk *forever* forming the idea instead of figuring out what is needed to get the idea to market.

There are many reasons new products, services, and technologies fail even when market research says they should allegedly succeed. They run out of money. They don't work as promised or at all. There is no ability to scale them. The company invests in the wrong sales and marketing—or not enough. The message does not resonate with consumers, or it fails to connect with different consumers. But for me, failure usually comes down to one factor: the inability to listen to and accept feedback. In short, if you don't listen to the market and other people, you won't master execution at the highest levels—period.

Vision can be a lonely, solitary space. You need people to challenge you, help you see what you can't see, bounce ideas off of, do what you can't, and be there when you can't—or don't want to—talk to anyone. People who lead with vision often have the capacity to bring others along with them. Just think about the biggest names in technology from the last generation: Gates, Jobs, Zuckerberg. They all loved to create, but to sell and grow their visions, they needed partners. They still did things their own way, but they were never alone.

Neither am I. My visions are driven by relationships. My leadership style is about collaboration and empowerment. Everyone around me has something to contribute to my visions. I want them to share my passion for them as much as I do—which is why mastering passion is the next step for mastering execution.

VISION CHECK
Questions for Self-Reflection

Have you ever had a vision that failed to come to fruition?

If so, why did it happen? Did you get lost in thinking? Miss or miscalculate the market? Think it was easier than it was to execute?

Lack commercial sense? Fail to connect with others? Or was it something else?

How would what you have learned about vision in this chapter have helped you? What would you have done differently?

How will you use what you learned in this chapter? What will you do differently?

Vision—Trait Summary and Real-Life Scenario

VISION: REFLECTIONS AND MOVING FORWARD

- Visions are North Stars—the things everything else in execution and in life revolve around. They are where you are going.

- Your vision will determine not only what you do in your life but also what you do with your life. You cannot allow your life to pass by default.

- Having a crystal-clear vision you can see and feel propels your actions.

- By taking charge of your North Star, being very clear about what you want, taking the necessary steps to execute it, and staying on track, you are setting yourself up for a life of greater success and fulfillment.

- You must always make sure that your vision is what *you* want. You must feel it, and it must be meaningful to you and congruent with who you are—not just what others think you should want.

- Bring your vision to life by visualizing what it would look like when you execute it at the highest level. Even if your vision is small, think big! (Just be careful that it's based somewhere in reality, not in wishful thinking.)

- Don't just think it. Ink it! Writing your vision and checkpoints or goals down makes you far more likely to succeed. Then, make sure you prioritize and reprioritize your actions to serve your vision.

- Remember: Vision can be a solitary and lonely space. Don't get lost in thinking.
- Make sure there is a market for what you envision, that your vision is not distracting you from the work needed to execute it, that you develop some commercial sense, and that you listen and connect with others who can give you feedback.

BEFORE YOU GO: WHAT'S THE SCENARIO?

This scenario is designed to help you think about everything you have learned in this section of the book. Please take a few minutes to complete this exercise the best you can. I promise it will be worth it. If you get stuck or you are not sure about your answer, go back and review the section. Remember, there is no right or wrong answer here. This is just a way to apply your new knowledge about vision.

Often it is easier to give advice to someone else, when you're not wrapped up in your own world, full of all its complexities. Picture this: Your colleague Brian confides in you that he wants to leave his job and go out on his own. You're worried for Brian because he has a family, no business plan, and little savings. At this point, all he has is an idea.

How would you use the concepts you've learned about vision to help him?

TRAIT 2

···

PASSION

What You're Willing to Sacrifice and Suffer For

*One person with passion is better
than forty people merely interested.*

—E. M. FORSTER

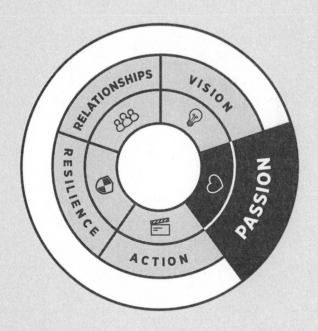

6

What We Do for Love

When I was 11, I fell in love with horseback riding. This was no childhood crush. I *loved* it. I had always loved horses and dreamed of riding. Before I was allowed to ride, my parents had given me a wood stump in the backyard to "act" as my horse. I cared for and fed that horse stump daily and "rode" it until they finally caved in and let me try riding. It was even better than I had imagined.

Every night after my first real rides, I would lie in my bed and close my eyes and envision myself in full equestrian gear astride a beautiful mare, the exhilarating soundlessness as we jumped, the excitement and power of the landing, the thrill of the cheers as we completed the course. But horseback riding lessons were expensive, and I had two siblings competing for their own activity funds. My parents said we could only afford two lessons a month at most, or it wouldn't be fair to my brother and sister.

Why does everything need to be fair? Why can't I be the kid that just gets to ride the horse? Can't they see how much I love this?

*Two lessons a month isn't going to cut it. If I wanted the skills to win competitions, I **needed** more lessons.*

I thought about begging, but I knew that wasn't going to work with two entrepreneur parents who expected us to earn everything we wanted. I asked my mom for help in coming up with a plan. She suggested talking to the owner to see if there was anything I could do to get more lessons.

I did and there was: I could clean the stables.

The deal was each day before I rode and any other time I could, I would clean out the horses' stalls. Seven hours of cleaning equaled one hour of lessons. I thought that was fair. Besides, what did I know about negotiation? Not that I would have been much of negotiator: I would have made the deal for double the hours because in my heart, this was what I wanted and needed to achieve my vision. I hated the work, but the lesson was clear, and I never forgot it:

**If you have passion for something,
you go out and make it happen—even if it
involves a lot of horse manure.**

I've been told that I make what I do look easy, but people don't see the thousands of nights and weekends I spend working. I don't talk about the conference calls I show up for when I am sick or the sleepless nights. I don't complain when I have to miss birthday parties or dinner dates or I have to change all my plans to fly halfway across the world. And my employees never knew I was worried about making payroll more than a dozen times. It was my passion that pushed me through these times.

Leading with Your Heart

Passion is about loving something so much you're willing to suffer for it. Passion doesn't make sleepless nights, stressful times, and hard work magically disappear, but it does make them bearable. It's what makes you go all in and keeps you there—no excuses. It's a fuel that pushes you to continue long after others have given up.

Those who lead with passion lead with their hearts. This passion is irresistible to others. I'm sure you can think of a time when you were persuaded by another person's enthusiasm to do or believe in something. This energy and enthusiasm is infectious, magnetic, and powerful. It drives engagement, innovation, resilience, and performance *in others and yourself—and encourages those around you to pursue and act with passion as well.*

This is why passion is the second trait you need to master for great execution. Action without passion is boring. It's mundane, everyday. It's changing a light bulb or doing laundry or washing dishes—necessary tasks we perform every day without even thinking or because we have to (even if we don't want to). These actions are largely humdrum and dispassionate, and they don't involve suffering or sacrifice.

That's the exact opposite of what you need to execute your vision.

What Passion Really Is

Remember: The word *passion* comes from the Latin root for suffering or enduring—a meaning somewhat disconnected from its modern application. To me, passion is closer to the word's original meaning: a form of pain that demands it be remedied. That's why I say passion is not just about doing the things you love or enjoy but also about doing the things that you would happily suffer for. You can't be 100 percent passionate 100 percent of the time. Some days my passion is more powerful than others. We're human, right? I strive to be at least 80 percent passionate 100 percent of the time. It may seem strange to put a number on it, but doing so sets a baseline for how I want to live my life.

"Just do the things you love" sounds like nice advice, but just doing the things you love is called a vacation. If you are suffering on vacation, you are doing something wrong, going to the wrong place, or bringing the wrong people. I may love sitting on the beach and drinking margaritas, but that doesn't mean I should be looking to turn it into a full-time career. I also love popcorn, fast cars, elephants, chardonnay, and 1980s music. Take those to a career counselor and see what you get!

Truth is, "love" is only one side of the passion coin. This book isn't another call to "follow your passions." This is a call to **master your passion**, and that mastery will require not only love but pain and sacrifice.

There's a big difference between those activities that you enjoy doing and those you would keep doing even when they became "painful," depleted your energy, and took up all your time. Just because you can sew doesn't mean you can succeed as a designer. Sure, you might love fashion and watch every episode of *Project Runway*. You might dream of designing clothes and even be inspired to knit or sew. But being a designer involves a whole set of skills and actions that go beyond an interest in clothes and producing a few garments. Being successful at it—like anything else—requires you to sacrifice and suffer for things that have nothing to do with fabric.

Loving what you do is one thing, but executing your vision to build a business and/or make a profit from it is another. You need to create a strategy and then refine it as you go. Suffer through the finances. Identify opportunities and market needs to find customers for what you are making (and deal with those customers). Market and advertise to help generate demand. Establish a social media presence. Deal with the setbacks and naysayers. And accept the inevitable rejection and criticism.

When I moved to Hawaii to build my business, more people told me I was crazy than wished me luck. *"There are no jobs there, Kim! The digital market is weak! Stay in LA and find something stable!"* I went anyway. While other people were off on vacation or going to parties, I was making one more product adjustment and perfecting the hundredth—yes, hundredth—version of my sales pitch.

When I went to Tahiti on my honeymoon in 2003, I wandered around Bora Bora looking for anywhere that had a computer with basic dial-up. I walked from my beautiful bungalow to a stuffy closet in the hotel office where I waited restlessly for an AOL connection to go through. I remember being on a safari in Africa watching a herd of elephants cross Kruger National Park . . . while I was on my phone to the office because that was the only place I had cell service.

"They want what to make the deal work? . . . Ooh, look at the elephants—they're amazing! . . . OK, tell them we need . . ."

Did I want to do any of that? Of course not! But my vision was my North Star, and my passion fueled my drive to achieve it—my passion to build the life that I wanted. I knew in my gut that everything I was doing felt right and that the pain I was enduring was part of what I needed to do to succeed. Passion justified any extreme work ethics that inevitably prioritized business over all other aspects of my life—often with really lousy timing, because I love spending time with people, on the beach, traveling the world, and exploring new cultures. Without that passion, I wouldn't have the stamina.

Many people just don't understand this. They don't see the sacrifice and suffering it takes to be successful. But that's what gives your success meaning! Thus, the starting point for finding your passion is not just in the things you love but in the things you would gladly suffer for.

Passion Pulse Check

Before you go any further, take a step back and ask yourself one question: *"Am I willing to suffer for this [idea, product, business, person, company]?"* If you answered no, take a step back before reading any further.

Figuring out what you're willing to suffer for
is hard. What will you give to get?

Passion isn't just fuel. It's the *emotional fuel* you need to execute at the highest level to achieve your vision and goals. Forget anything you have been told about suppressing emotions and being unemotional in your work. It's not realistic. It's a lie that eventually traps you. Why would you want to be unemotional about what you spend most of every day doing? You need to *feel* what you are doing and then learn how to make others feel it too.

Execution is all about *mastering* your passion and creating that emotional connection to your goals and vision. It fuels learning, memory, and focus. It provides everything you need to persevere, endure, act, connect with and attract others to your vision. Without this emotional connection, you're just a moment away from being bored and distracted and, ultimately, from failing.

What does it mean to be emotionally connected to something? What do you feel? How do you act? That's the next step in understanding passion and how it helps drive execution.

PASSION CHECK
Questions for Self-Reflection

Driving forward with passion is a huge part of your success in execution. Answer these questions before you move to the next chapter to better understand the depth of your passion:

- Does your vision reflect what you are most passionate about?

If you answered no, answer the following questions before answering the final question below:

- What are you truly passionate about? A subject (fashion, food, animals)? A skill (creating, writing)? A role (leader, teacher, caretaker)? Something else?
- Which of these do you feel most emotionally connected to?

- Which of these are you most willing to "suffer" for? What would you want to keep doing even if you had to give something up or didn't get paid or acknowledged?

If you answered yes to the first question or if you have now identified what you're passionate about, answer this question: *How will you remind yourself of that passion during the long hours?*

7

Emotional Rescue

When I got fired from my first dot-com, I was devastated. I loved the company, loved the people, and loved what I was doing. I was upset not just because of the fear of having no income but because I had lost a job I felt emotionally connected to. I was embarrassed.

I remember calling my dad, and his response was, "I told you this was going to happen. They were spending beyond their means and income. It was inevitable, Kimmy."

Even though this was the truth, my dad's words were not what I needed to hear. I already felt terrible, and was calling him to console me. He was cold and callous.

How many times have you been that person? The person who asks for sympathy and gets none? I'd like to think I've never missed the opportunity to try to make people feel better, but I know I have. Instead, I've given in to my knee-jerk reaction and said, "I told you so!" But that's the last thing anyone would want in my dot-com situation. We'd want kindness. Without that kindness, the other person risks twisting the knife. The only reason I was so upset is because I *cared* about what I was doing—I had an emotional connection to it. Yet so often, like my dad, the other person we need to be kind fails to understand this.

"What do you want me to say?" the other person pleads.

Nothing. We want you to say *nothing*. At that moment, we just want a hug from Dad, a partner, a friend. We want to know everything is OK. We want to know you care:

- How many times have we been "that person" when it comes to dealing with the inevitable mistakes, failures, and problems when executing our visions?
- How many times have we been "that person" and told someone or told ourselves the best thing to do in that moment is say, "Get yourself together now, and look at what you've done wrong."
- How many times have we been "that person" and told ourselves or had someone tell us, "Calm down! Don't get so upset! Stop being so emotional. Here's why you screwed up."

Yes, it's smart to calm down before you explain a mistake to your boss or team. Your explanation will be more sincerely received when you've taken the time to relax and be thoughtful and reflective on what went wrong. What's important to remember is not to suppress what feels true to you. Don't deny your emotions a chance to teach you a lesson. Don't run away from feelings or rationalize emotions away. Doing those things is to deny the passion that will fuel the next attempt and the next. *Let those emotions out— give them your ear and a figurative or, if appropriate, a literal hug!*

Why Emotions Are Critical to Passion

Emotions are what drive our passion, and those feelings are critical to leading a full life. This is why action without passion leaves us empty—we may get stuff done, but the results will only satisfy us temporarily. Emotions force us to feel actions we stand behind.

Your passion for something is what inspires, engages, and connects you to the people around you. There are two sides to this coin, however. On the one side, people who are not engaged by your passion may not be the right people to surround yourself with because you don't share the same vision in order to execute together. On the other, if you are not demonstrating that passion, then they have no reason to feel a connection to you and your vision and execute for you.

Beware of dismissing all this as "soft stuff." This is about being authentic and true to your vision. Your passion must have meaning, or the consequences can be dire. Consider this: We can easily ignore or not even see objects that have no meaning for us. In one study, commercial pilots landed their planes on top of another in a flight simulation because they didn't see the other plane—a scenario they would be highly unlikely to encounter in real life. This is called "inattentional blindness."[1]

When it comes to execution, it's not just about visualizing your vision but feeling a deep connection to the visions we are executing. Emotions move us. They impact our behavior and thoughts. If we are angry, we fight and yell. If we are sad, we cry. If we are happy, we laugh and dance. The joy I had when I was 11 years old being around horses made me indifferent to the fact that I was cleaning stables. Similarly, the passion I have for what I'm doing and the people I am working with today move me to be willing to work late and travel often. I never forget that my head (reason and logic) and heart (emotion and passion) must coexist.

Passion Pulse Check

Think about one thing in your past you have been passionate about or emotionally connected to. How successful were you at this endeavor? Why do you think that was?

Now, think about something in your past you have done from a place of logic or reason rather than an emotional connection. How successful were you at this endeavor? Why do you think that was?

Emotions may be unpredictable and uncontrollable, but understanding and mastering those emotions so they drive you but don't push you over the edge is key to mastering passion and successful execution. I know we all like to think we're rational and logical, but the fact is that emotions drive us, and sometimes they veer in different directions. Ideally, we use logic to devise our strategies, but we need emotion to fuel our passion to carry them out.

Yes, this runs contrary to what many books say, that it is better to elevate reason and logic and discount feelings. Reason is powerful, but emotions are *what matter most*. If you're going to suffer for what you love, you need to feel it—the highs and lows—not repress it.

Why Passion Is Critical to Success

When my mother-in-law was diagnosed with early-onset Alzheimer's at 65, I was determined to find a way to help her. I knew I couldn't cure the disease, but I was committed to finding a way she could live her best and most comfortable life. I researched day and night. Eastern medicine, Western medicine, brain games, studies, diets. I even tried a noninvasive medical device that stimulates the brain, but when I tried it on myself first, it overstimulated my brain and I shut down for two days. I couldn't leave my bed, focus, or concentrate.

My fierce love for my mother-in-law awakened a passion in me to learn more about brain health to try to help her in any way I could. I asked a doctor friend whose husband had a brain tumor what they would recommend. She said the two of them, both Stanford MDs, had been taking a variety of supplements to help increase their mental clarity and memory, and I asked if they could make me a sample. They agreed. Grateful and more determined than ever, I enlisted a partner I knew could help. After a year of tireless work and research with the doctors, we created supplements to increase brain activity. My emotional connection and desire to help my mother-in-law was critical in their creation.

While most visions will not be driven by serious disease, they are driven by some kind of call to action, and they benefit from a continued high level of emotional connection to your vision, goals, and actions. That connection drives almost everything: positivity, self-belief, learning, focus, memory, satisfaction, and above all, motivation. This has several important implications highlighting the benefits of passion that are dismissed when it comes to business, leadership, and execution:

- Passion drives self-belief.
- Passion stimulates motivation.
- Passion influences learning.
- Passion maintains levels of energy and enthusiasm.
- Passion inspires others.

Passion Drives Self-Belief

To be successful, your confidence must be greater than everyone else's doubt. People who have passion are emotionally connected and thus really believe that they will be successful. This belief permeates their entire being and inspires confidence in themselves and others.

Imagine a coach talking to the team just before they leave the locker room. At that moment, will the coach go over all the tactical details, or will he or she passionately deliver a rousing speech designed to fire up the team and their self-belief? No one executes on a vision saying, "I think I can lose" or "Everyone thinks I can't do it, so I shouldn't even try."

Passion Stimulates Motivation

It's a biological fact that more emotion—more passion—equals more motivation. Our fight-or-flight reflex is the perfect example of this. But it happens in less dangerous or high-stakes situations every day too. Our brains are wired in such a way that higher levels of emotion literally stimulate the motivational areas of the brain. If we're really excited about something—a trip, a pitch, an idea—we're likely to have many more positive thoughts and want to act. Similarly, if we feel that high level of passion from someone else, we are motivated to follow.

The best example of this is seeing people in front of you taste something delicious. You can see in their eyes how much they love it. It's a visceral reaction, and that emotional response and our instinctive empathic connection to it makes us want to act to have the same dish or steal some of theirs!

Passion Influences Learning

Think of your favorite teachers in school. I bet they were the ones who were the most passionate about the subjects they taught. The teacher who made biology fun. The English professor who brought a story to life. The math teacher who took the extra time to apply problems to real life in a way you understood.

That was certainly true for me. Growing up, I loved my marketing and math classes and the teachers who taught them. Looking back, if I had teachers with the same enthusiasm in science and English, I wonder if I would have excelled equally and perhaps taken a different career path.

Passion Maintains Levels of Energy and Enthusiasm

Most people typically underestimate what is required for tasks and the time it will take to complete them. That work can also be quite repetitive—even boring. Without emotion and passion to carry you through the setbacks, you will feel blocked from your path.

That's when passion keeps you going—not just when you face obstacles (as we will see when we get to resilience) or sleepless nights. It's when you are faced with the most ordinary tasks and need to remember why you are there, or when you are in another uninspiring meeting and need to lift the room around you.

Which brings me to my final point.

Passion Inspires Others

Passion is contagious. We are programmed to sense and even copy levels of energy, so your passion can inspire and influence others as well as discourage detractors. It will influence how they see you as well as how they see themselves. Because your passion isn't only about you. It isn't, "I'm excited!" It's, "I'm excited, and here is my vision and how you can play a part in it!"

You need to be vulnerable enough to open yourself up to others so they can fully appreciate your passion and vision. That will be key when we get to the relationships. Because when you are truly passionate about something, it reveals an authenticity about how you show up in the world. As I said in the opening of this book, authenticity is key to executing on your vision—especially when it comes to passion.

You can fake knowledge. You can fake skills. But can you fake passion? No. How can you fake something that

- Drives your belief in a successful outcome.
- Accelerates memory and learning.
- Stimulates motivation.
- Maintains levels of energy and enthusiasm.
- Energizes and inspires others.

I used to think I needed to change my "frequency" to be like others. I'd dial myself and my frequency down to *theirs*. The result? I'd end up spending time with people who had nothing in common with me or the vision of the life I wanted to live. I quickly felt like I didn't belong, draining me of my energy and passion. Pretending to be someone I wasn't was *exhausting*. It was a character I never wanted to play. Over the years, I learned to embrace my truth and everything I've been called: rebellious, a bad influence, a nonconformist. If someone told me I couldn't do something, I would do it anyway. I place more importance on what I expect of myself than on what others expect of me. I'm more values driven than rules driven. My life will never be traditional, and I'm okay with that.

People trying to sell you "fake" passion will always expose themselves eventually. The façade will crumble, and you will know their hearts aren't in it. It's like that law in physics: every action has an equal and opposite reaction. Once you don't believe that they will suffer and sacrifice for their visions, you won't believe that they will suffer and sacrifice for *you*.

Think about a colleague, leader, or mentor who you felt was driven by passion. What impact did that have on you? Do you have that same impact on others? That emotional engagement is key!

Be fearless to act so people believe
your passion is leading to something,
and you execute together.

Don't be in neutral when it comes to passion, or you'll just be mismanaging your expectations. I'm passionate about people and helping others, letting people pursue their passions for new directions and opportunities, and people helping me see what I don't know.

Passion Pulse Check

Ask yourself right now: "On a scale from 1 to 10, how deeply do I feel an emotional connection to what I am doing?" If it is anything lower than an 8, how and why do you expect to execute at the highest level? How do you expect those around you to feel it and do the same?

A Word of Warning:
Not All Passion Looks the Same

Executing with passion or even being emotional about something doesn't mean you have to jump up and down with excitement and energy. Just because people aren't yelling doesn't mean they aren't angry. Just because people aren't crying doesn't mean they aren't sad. You don't need extremes to feel a connection to what you are doing, which means you don't have to be extroverted and outgoing to execute and lead with passion. In fact, some of the most successful people were or are notoriously introverted like Bill Gates, Steven Spielberg, and Eleanor Roosevelt.

People manifest their emotions differently. The key is that you feel emotionally and congruently connected—which will come across in everything you do. Passion is about how you feel and what others feel from you, and you don't need to bounce off the walls to do that.

That said, just because people *are* bouncing off the walls doesn't mean they are not in control of their passions. Exhibiting emotionality does not make someone irrational. If it did, I would have been institutionalized rather than appointed as the CEO every time I sold my company. I tend to be a high-energy person most of the time, but I don't need to temper my passion to be thoughtful or open to logical considerations and viable alternatives. That I tend to get very excited about things I am passionate about, which I express through my words as well as my body language, does not mean I am out of control.

I realize, however, that there is always a risk that people will interpret my bubbly exterior as a lack of depth and intelligence. The expression of passion is relative. If I am enthusiastic about everything, it can undermine my authenticity with people I want to help execute my vision. People always have an emotional response to how you act, and you must be aware of how you're being perceived. That self-awareness is a strength.

As I said before, I have my own "frequency," but I *must* appreciate others' frequencies and accept their perception of mine. Over time I have learned to keep my frequency, maybe modulating it when necessary out of decorum but *never* changing it completely. I won't water down my passion around people who don't act the same way I do or who I think cannot appreciate or understand it. I need them to see the real me and know that what they see is what they get.

Besides, they may be looking for that very difference in someone to work with—something that complements their passion, not mimics it. I know I am. I don't want someone in my life—at work or at home—who is like me. I want people who do what I can't and make me appreciate things I normally wouldn't see or do myself. I understand who I am. I have succeeded by staying true to my North Star and my passion for it, not aiming at what others wanted that North Star to be. Why would I then expect someone else to change for me? I'd rather stand by myself and appreciate differences in others by encouraging them to do the same so that we can execute and succeed together as a team.

To understand this further, try this exercise:

- For one day, within all your interactions, look for passion in others. What do you notice? When are you aware of the passion others have? How does it make you feel? What do you notice about their passion? How could you better appreciate that passion and allow it to thrive alongside yours?

I love being around people who believe in me, who feel a connection and are excited and energetic. The energy is contagious. That's what passion feeds on: energy.

PASSION CHECK

Questions for Self-Reflection

Have you ever been told, "Don't let your emotions get the better of you?" Have you regretted ignoring a passion because you rationalized it away as frivolous?

How do you show when you are emotionally connected to something? How does it change your behavior?

How have people responded to you when you are passionate?

How do you respond to passion? Do you have a bias toward people who act emotionally?

These are essential questions to reflect on to understand how emotion fuels passion and thus successful execution because you are willing to do whatever it takes.

8

Fueling Your Fire

Driven by Passion, CEO Sells $235 Million Company from Middle of the Ocean.

That would be the headline if I were writing my own story about the sale of my company in 2014. Sounds like a good story, right? It was. But like all good stories, it involved more time than I anticipated and a lot of sacrifice, especially for my husband.

The year before the sale. My husband and I were traveling to Bali for our 10-year anniversary when I made an unscheduled stopover in Singapore to meet the head of a potential acquiring company for a drink. Did my husband want to stop in Singapore for our 10-year anniversary? Probably not. But he saw the look on my face. He felt my passion as I explained why. He knew this had to be something big—not just in my mind but in my heart.

Those drinks turned to dinner with our spouses followed by brunch the next morning with their kids. We really hit it off, and I knew we would be a great fit. They were entrepreneurial and innovative, and based on our short time together, I just knew they would be the perfect home for my company.

Once I got back from Singapore, I wrote down my vision to sell my company on a note I stuck to my bathroom mirror. I wanted that vision staring at me every morning and night, reinforcing my passion and strengthening my resolve to weather what I needed to do to close the deal.

Six months later, we still hadn't closed the deal. My husband and I were now on a scheduled sailing trip, and I found myself trying to get a call to go through on a satellite phone to keep the deal moving.

Much to my husband's disappointment, the satellite phone worked. I could hear him calling me in the background.

"Are you still talking business?"

Yes, yes, I was. It could have been seasickness or deal fatigue, but I was getting dispirited. My vision posted on my bathroom mirror was 3,000 miles away. I had even started to doubt myself, but my passion pushed the doubt aside.

That's what passion does. It pushes you through those moments when you need to make unpopular decisions or hard choices. While it's not always easy, there are benefits of being obsessively passionate about your business. The hard part is, what happens after years and years of being passionate and making those sacrifices, when even the new seems a little old and you're tired of missing another family dinner?

Clearly, passion is essential for success, so it is critical that you nurture it and stay connected to fuel your fire. I have talked about how articulating your vision and keeping it in mind are essential, just as I did with that note on my mirror to sell my company. The same is true for your passion.

There are two important ways to do this:

- Fostering your passion
- Prioritizing your passion

Fostering Your Passion

In interviews, people often ask me, "What is your hobby?" They might be looking for me to say tennis, art, or hiking. I tell them the truth: my hobby is my passion for helping others achieve their dreams, and I foster it by helping people execute to be successful. It's why I built my company and hired back many of the people I had to lay off in my first job when the tech bubble burst. It's why I became an active angel investor and always take calls from entrepreneurs looking for advice.

When I tell people my hobby, they always say something like, "Jeez, you never take a break from work." While it's hard to do in some ways, none of it feels like work for me. This is my passion— and it's the very thing that fuels me and energizes me. Fostering my passion by spending time helping people gives me energy to operate in every other facet of my life with passion, and creates a healthy work-life integration. Not work-life separation.

What are you doing regularly that
fuels your passion?

Are you doing things on a day-to-day basis that fuel your passions? Maybe you're like me and work *is* your passion—or at least one of them. What could you do to foster your passion in order to execute?

- Maybe you're passionate about fashion and could start writing a blog.
- Maybe you're passionate about kids and education and could volunteer at a school in your area.
- Maybe your passion is yoga, and instead of just doing yoga, you could find a class and get certified so you could teach it.
- Maybe you're passionate, the way I am, about business and people, and you could join a local or national entrepreneurs' organization or start one with a group of friends.
- Maybe you're looking to advance in your company and could ask your boss about taking a leadership course.

Passion Pulse Check

Choose a passion that you have, and bring this passion to life for a day. How does that make you feel? What impact does this have on your energy and motivation?

The point is to do something, whatever it is, for you. Don't worry about whether someone will say no, especially at work. Most leaders understand that employees want to be engaged and passionate and make a difference. Because passionate employees make the best employees. Leaders will be glad you took the initiative—you can't expect others to foster your passion for you.

Remember: Even if you are a business of one, you are your own employee whom you need to take care of. Make yourself and your passion a priority.

Prioritizing Your Passion

Phil Molyneux is an Englishman with a French name who moved to the United States in 2010 to work for a Japanese company. That's when Sony asked him to lead its electronics business in the United States. After three years in Budapest running the company's business in Central and Southeast Europe, he wanted to make an immediate and genuine impact on the people he was about to lead who knew nothing about him.

He decided the best way to do that was to meet with them all before he started . . . individually. *All 1,200 of them.*

Before his official start date in the United States, over three full days, Phil stopped at every occupied desk bottom floor to top at the Sony headquarters in San Diego and chatted for a minute or so. He did this because he authentically wanted people to know who he was and what he stood for, that he cared about who they were and what they stood for, and that he truly valued open, honest communication.

That's what Phil had a passion for—authenticity, connection, and communication—and he made it his priority in meeting with 1,200 people in three days.

I talked about prioritizing and reprioritizing your vision to the top of the list. The same is true for your passion. A hundred things are going to come at you each day. But you need to keep pushing your passion and vision back to the top of the list. You need to prioritize both time and energy to foster your passion.

*This has as much to do with saying **yes** to your passion as saying **no** to the things you're not passionate about. But it also means saying **no** to things you want to do so you can prioritize your passion. There are trade-offs no matter what.*

Saying no is never easy, which is why prioritizing passion and quality time for your vision are so difficult to deliver on. There will never be enough time to do everything you want and need to do. Prepare yourself to disappoint people as you decline invitations to attend birthday parties, potlucks, or dinners with friends. This goes for all parts of your life! For me, when I am done with work, my family is my priority. That means skipping out on happy hours with my girlfriends to finish what I need to do in the office so that I am fully present at the dinner table that night with my husband and kids. I will opt for a lunch with a close friend instead of a dinner that goes late, no matter how much fun those can be.

But none of this works if I'm not transparent with the people whom this affects. If I need to be somewhere far away to achieve my broader vision of a great life and miss a few family dinners or disrupt a vacation that is crucial to my vision, I will carve out time. My husband knows when those things are a priority. I write down my top priorities each week to keep them fresh in my mind, and put them in a place where we both can see them. Transparency! That's why my husband understood when the sale of my company disrupted our vacation. He knew what my priorities were because I had shared them with him, and he in turn supported me throughout the process.

Do the people around you know when you are prioritizing your passion? They are the ones who will help you mitigate feelings of guilt and doubt when you've missed the third New Year's Eve party in a row—and it will ensure the people you're not seeing don't feel you just don't like them. Don't let them assume. I make it a point to let the people closest to me always know how important they are to me by being fully present in everything I do. For example, my friends and family aren't offended when I don't make it to big parties because I prefer intimate, quality time with smaller groups or one-on-ones. I may have skipped out on that late dinner with my friend, but at our next catch-up lunch, I had my phone tucked in my bag the entire time. No distractions except our own laughter and excitement to talk about as much as we could.

Being fully present in everything you do is one of the keys to work-life integration. Separating work and home life is often impossible these days, and if you truly love what you do, it's not a chore to take a 7 a.m. call on the weekend or devote some of your vacation time to business. Just prioritize correctly so that your quality time always goes toward people and projects you love.

The only thing no one has learned to make more of is **time**. Maintaining a million friendships, a family, and a business is impossible. Decide which aspects of your life are priorities, and scale back on the rest. Find trustworthy people whom you can hand off tasks to. You need to leave time for essentials—like sleep!

I can remember sitting for hours and hours among thousands of data servers in a freezing underground data center in downtown Los Angeles to ensure we would complete our next code release in time. I couldn't actually help, because I don't code, but I had to be there nonetheless. The guy doing it was a genius but was often unable to stay focused enough to meet deadlines. As a result, there I was, next to him to ensure that the deadline was met. It was. However, in terms of running my business, I paid a steep price. The opportunity cost of not being able to spend my time on other things as I sat there shivering and essentially useless to the task was high—and unhealthy. I learned that day I was

never going to succeed unless I found more personally accountable individuals who are able to continually execute.

But heed one more word of warning: you must allow yourself
time for celebrating those achievements with those individuals
along the way. You may want to skip all the fun, but prioritizing
and fostering passion can't be only about the continuous grind
or you'll burn out. Don't be that person who has forgotten what
fun is!

Productive Passion: Celebrate Good Times—Come On!

Before he became a Hall of Fame speaker helping teams and
their leaders become peak performers in business, Walter Bond
dreamed of playing in the National Basketball Association (NBA).
Odds were slim. But he kept practicing and working hard, pursuing his passion to achieve his vision. He ended up realizing the
first step when the University of Minnesota recruited him and
he . . . rode the bench. At the end of his first year, Walter asked
his coach, "What do I need to do to be an NBA player?" He said,
"Look son, you don't even play for *me!*"

But Walter's passion for his vision was undeterred. He was
relentless. He attacked the list his coach gave him to better his
game. Every year in Minnesota he was voted the Most Improved
Player—until his senior year. When he broke his foot. Twice. His
prospects of playing in the NBA went from seemingly none to
"Walter Who?"

Still, Walter's passion was undeterred. He went back to his
coach and said, "What do I need to do to play in the NBA?" The

coach told Walter he should be a motivational speaker. "Coach, I can talk the rest of my life, but I have only one chance to play basketball professionally. Tell me, what do I need to do be an NBA player?" The coach told him to lose 20 pounds and learn to knock down a three-point shot. Over the next two months, he got in great shape, worked on his shot, and transformed himself from an unknown college reserve to an NBA prospect.

In November 1992, Walter Bond became the first-ever undrafted rookie free agent to start for the NBA's Dallas Mavericks on opening day. He played in the NBA for several years after that and then in Germany for several more before retiring and becoming the acclaimed motivational speaker his college coach predicted.

But while Walter played, something changed in him. He could have kept pushing every moment during the season and straight into the off-season, always asking, "What's next?" And he did push himself hard. But before he pushed, he learned the power of taking a mental step back. Every night before he ran out on the court, he listened as the announcer said his name to the fans, "At six feet five inches tall weighing 215 pounds, from the University of Minnesota . . . Walter Bond!" He made himself stop and say, "Dude, I'm *here*. I *made* it. Kids all over the world would love to have my jersey. Players all over the world would love to have my job. I got here!"

I love Walter's story and the lesson it teaches us:

Celebrating the small wins is about more than closing a chapter on the past or acknowledging the success of the team. It's a checkpoint on your vision, and it marks a new beginning for everyone, including you, to fuel your passion, keep winning, and achieve even more.

In business and life, we spend way too much time obsessing over our failures, deconstructing them—even celebrating them as badges of honor. This distraction is not healthy or productive. Why don't we celebrate the successes?

Answer this question: aside from an actual celebration like a holiday party or a wedding or the end of something big like closing a huge deal, when was the last time you focused on telling yourself that you did a great job? Just a pat on the back followed by nothing negative. No list of the things that you could have done and a to-do list for the week ahead. No next steps for executing. Just a "Great job!" Few people I know can remember a time off the top of their heads.

That's because we're far more likely to do it with our pets than ourselves or other people. But that's not unusual: Many people have a tough time taking compliments and deflect them with lines like, "Thanks, but I could have done better" or "Great, but there's more to do!" or "I'm happy you're pleased, but I can't stop now."

Is celebrating a small win really a sign of weakness or an excuse for not doing more? Too often people say, "I can't do that" or "I don't have time to celebrate," when they really mean, "I won't take the time." That's cutting yourself off from your passion. You need to start small and build from there:

- Love cooking dinner for your family? Pick a *night* to start, not a whole week.
- Want to travel? Skip the weeklong production and get an inexpensive hotel room in the nearest city for a weekend.
- Love the movies? Go to a midday matinee of that movie you've been dying to see—and go ahead and splurge on a tub of warm popcorn.

Celebrating is a choice, and it's an important one. You should say no to distractions when prioritizing your passion, but you must also make celebrating a priority. You deserve it. As my grandmother always said, everything in moderation, including moderation.

Is every small win worthy of celebration? Yes! It's just about scaling your celebration to match the performance and rekindling your passion. The most centered professional athletes know to celebrate every win on the field in a public way in front of the fans—home or away. It doesn't matter if it is a win against the last-place team or a major upset. They celebrate the small wins, not just the championships, before moving on to the next game. That's about perspective and enjoying what you do—both big parts of what I call *productive passion*.

Without productive passion, you will not only lose sight of your North Star but also lose steam.

With passion as my fuel, I have chosen to apply myself in the cut and thrust of business, and I let my achievements speak for themselves. I can't just keep saying no to the things and people I love—at work and at home—and not expect that fuel to be depleted. Whatever you want to do, you want to make a difference. Wherever it is you want to end up, let passion be the fuel for your vision to get you there. Remember: You won't reach those destinations if you are not fully present in life.

Most of us have experienced moments when our talents were fully engaged—when we rose to a challenge and were making a difference. The great psychologist Mihaly Csikszentmihalyi calls this a state of "flow": a mental state of complete absorption in the current experience. Achieving a state of flow means taking the time to remember the joy and purpose behind your vision so you don't end up alone, buried by work, with sanity being a distant memory. U.S. businesses shell out hundreds of millions of dollars each year to achieve employee engagement, and spend billions developing employees' skill sets. Yet only 13 percent of the workforce attests to having the right type of passion—the kind that drives employees to seek out challenges and develop the skills to push past them.[1] That's unfortunate because productive passion and its resulting commitment may improve the health of your people and even your own health. A study conducted in Denmark found that out of 5,000 Danish workers, those with the highest commitment to their employers slept better and got sick less.[2]

Passion Pulse Check

The next time you hit a small goal on the way to a big one? Celebrate it with a toast, and own that win. Pat yourself on the back. Smile. Laugh. Go home and play with your kids. Take your significant other out on a date. Buy your team some wine and cheese, and invite them to your place during a work afternoon.

Doing those things will not mean you have taken your eye off the ultimate goal. They simply allow you to recharge, boost morale, and connect emotionally, and they serve as checkpoints along the way to execution and your ultimate success.

Even if you don't get sick or burn out, just keeping your nose to the proverbial grindstone can get you stuck—and getting stuck in passion is probably the saddest of all. Imagine if you gave up on your passion only because you were exhausted or couldn't find your way forward. That's when you need to tell yourself or tell your people to stop. Go home. Take a wellness day.

It's a simple equation: you must be productively passionate to have productively passionate employees. Passionate employees are loyal and happy employees. Loyal and happy employees are what you want your clients and customers—everyone who comes in contact with you and your business—to see. You can't do that without that flow in all parts of your life.

> How much does it take you
> to never call in sick? How much will it
> cost you to never call in well?

And when you get the big wins—the championships!—make sure you throw yourself and everyone around a celebration worthy of the triumph. For example, when we had our first $1 million month at my first company, we celebrated with a team trip to Vegas. More than 10 years later, I took my team to Tokyo for two days when we reached an even bigger goal so that I could deliver on my promise to sing karaoke in the *Lost in Translation* booth. The team rallied around my challenge. It created camaraderie, and our passion drove us to achieve our shared vision.

The passion others feel for your passion while also pursuing their own is what builds great companies and helps realize great visions.

My sister calls me the "Lighthouse CEO": I have to light up everything around me. But I can't do it all at once, so whatever

I'm looking at is what I'm focused on until I need to move to the next thing, always illuminating all my passions around me. People feel it too. When I'm looking at them, I try illuminating them with my passion, hoping we can shine brightly together. For that moment, we are 100 percent present and focused—it's a two-way street of shared purpose. That's how productive passion inspires action. It makes everyone able to act and react with confidence that the boat will reach the shore so everyone can take the next steps *together*.

PASSION CHECK

Questions for Self-Reflection

On a scale of 1 to 10, how good are you at doing things that foster your passions?

In what ways could you better foster your passions?

How are you going to prioritize your passions to help you keep executing?

On a scale of 1 to 10, how good are you at celebrating the small wins?

What could you do *now* for yourself, your family, or your coworkers to make that happen or keep it happening?

9

Never Completely Submit to the Dark Side

My dad spent 30 years in Portland, Oregon, chasing his dream of rehabilitating housing to restore neighborhoods to the family communities they had once been. He built 300 homes, which together would be worth close to $100 million today—*if* he hadn't sold all of them over a 15-year period to fund his new vision for changing the face of elder care.

Unfortunately, that elder care venture proved to be more difficult and costly than he had originally planned. A long-term vision often requires a degree of faith and risk to go with your pain and suffering, especially if it involves creating or reinventing a market for a product or service. The lesson is that my dad's passion blinded him to this risk. Just as he does when he gambles, he kept going even when prudence said to stop and take a step back and reevaluate. He just kept going, never realizing how deep he had gotten. He ended up selling all his homes to fuel his passion and fund his new vision.

My dad never saw how deep he was going and how it was affecting more than his financial security—it was affecting his entire life, including us, his family. It was as if he had stepped into quicksand. He loved all of us, but he had been consumed by the dark side of passion: his willingness to suffer blinded him to all his problems. He just kept pushing through the pain—kept pushing forward. He forgot to take a step back. He failed to take stock of what he did and didn't know.

He forgot to master his passion. When he didn't take the necessary steps to demarcate how much he was willing to sacrifice, it affected him both monetarily and personally.

Pain can be productive and necessary when it comes to passion, but it can lead you to focus on the wrong things and ignore other problems, warning signs, people, possibilities, opportunities, and ideas. No other trait has such a deep dark side.

Be a Passion Jedi

Finding your passion empowers you to stretch yourself as an entrepreneur and ensures your business's growth. It's an emotional force that can be harnessed for incredible success. That strong emotional connection to your goals and dreams is a powerful drive, but it can also result in inflexibility—an inability to adjust and correct course. People who lead with passion can struggle to keep their goals in mind and can tend to take setbacks personally. Don't worry, we're all human, and I can certainly relate. A high level of passion and belief in ourselves will push us to go to seemingly unimaginable lengths, but we must make sure our passion does not inhibit or blind us at the same time to realities or to the need to adapt and evolve.

There are plenty of examples of brands and companies that collapsed or have struggled because their passions blinded them to the market's reality and they failed to adapt—Kodak, BlackBerry, and Blockbuster, to name a few. But I want you to consider pain one more time from a personal level.

The chapters in this section have described some of the warning signs that passion was blinding me and others:

- I didn't negotiate for a better deal for my horseback riding lessons because I would have done even more work to get them, so I just said yes to the first offer.
- Passion in extremes can lead others to see you as irrational and illogical, which will cause them to dismiss you and your ideas.
- Passion can make it difficult to choose what and whom to focus on and make it difficult to identify your highest priorities.
- Passion can make you forget to stop from time to time and smell the roses and celebrate.

Before we continue to action, I want you to stop and audit yourself when it comes to passion. You can't lose yourself in the dark side and expect to execute or help others execute at the highest level.

This is about you.

My grandmother told me to take care of my husband first before my kids because if my husband was happy, then my kids would be happy. While she was right about many things, I think she was wrong with that one (sorry, Grandma). It's really about you being good to *you* first. If I'm good at home, I can be good to others, my family is good, and my work is good too. Makes sense, right? If I'm good when I'm in the office, then so are my employees. If my employees are good, then they are giving me more time to be with my family. This is a big reason why people who lead with passion can have trouble working with people who don't drive from the heart—people who are "just doing their jobs." Your passion is intertwined with theirs, and the jobs are rarely separated.

To ensure that you resist the darkest side of passion like a passion Jedi, ask yourself questions like these:

- Do I say yes to requests and ideas too quickly?
- Am I mastering my passion and manifesting it productively, or is it controlling me?
- Am I *still* passionate about what I'm doing? Does it still make me happy?
- Am I focusing on the right things and people? Are they still things and people I'm willing to suffer for?
- Has what I am passionate about changed or evolved and I haven't?
- Do I need to let go and try new things? Do I need to do things differently? Pursue less obvious choices?

Don't just ask these questions in moments of self-reflection when things are going wrong. Even when things are calm, you should reflect. It's also important to ask questions when you can't stop, or won't stop, acting and executing. You need to know that what you are doing feels right, that you trust the direction your passion and the team are pulling you in, and that you are still aligned with your vision—that you can and should keep going.

I've always had great admiration for TV shows that go out while they are on top and are executing on the highest level, before their passion flagged, such as *M*A*S*H*, *Cheers!*, *Friends*, and *Seinfeld*.

Now, ask yourself one more question: "Am I remembering to have fun even when I feel the pain?"

I know too many leaders who refuse to take and bask in the love and only try to give. They send the team out for a drink but refuse to go along. They order lunch for the office but don't join in. They ask how their employees are doing but never share how they are. They send their employees to a spa but never go themselves. They make someone take a day off but won't use their own vacation time.

You can't just be good to others. You need to be good to yourself and let others be good to you. You might think you're being humble, but actually you're making it about you because the focus will be on you as the team wonders why you won't spend time with them.

Stop letting your passion drive you away from others. Join that team for lunch. Go to the celebratory happy hour. Take a well day or a vacation, and share with the team what you did.

············

Live a passion-powered life. Lose yourself in a life you love and share it with others.

············

Simply put, it starts with you. If you are not good with your passion, then no one else will be—and remember you can't fake it! Make sure you are living your passion and you are enabling and empowering others to live theirs, doing what is genuine to them, not just to you. We like to celebrate together, but we also like to be individuals celebrating and living out loud in our own ways. This is the way I live, day in, day out. Passion is the driver of everything I've ever achieved (and will achieve!) and the amazing and blessing-filled life that I am living. Where will your passion take you?

PASSION CHECK

Questions for Self-Reflection

Remember: Passion in execution is about doing those things you are emotionally connected to and willing to suffer for. It's what you need to drive you through the long hours, unexpected obstacles, and all the challenges that must be overcome to execute effectively and realize your goals.

If you haven't already, please take the time to carry out the actions and complete the self-reflection exercises in this section:

- What have you learned about passion and execution?
- What have you learned about yourself in this section?
- Have you ever let the darkest side of passion—the pain— blind you?
- What will you now do differently?

Passion—Trait Summary and Real-Life Scenario

PASSION: REFLECTIONS AND MOVING FORWARD

- Passion is loving what you do so much you are willing to suffer for it—it is the fuel needed in execution to achieve your vision and goals and to execute at the highest level.

- Anything worth doing involves difficulties, challenges, and setbacks. Passion doesn't make sleepless nights, stressful times, and hard work magically disappear, but it does make them bearable.

- Passion is the emotional connection to your vision.

- This level of emotion is necessary because it drives almost everything: positivity, self-belief, learning, focus, satisfaction, and motivation.

- Those who lead with passion lead with their hearts. Their energy and enthusiasm are infectious, and they drive engagement, innovation, resilience, and high performance in themselves and others.

- Remember those others and yourself when you are fostering and prioritizing your passion to take the time to care for you and celebrate with others.

- But beware! This strong emotional connection to your goals and dreams is a powerful drive, but it can also be misinterpreted as irrational and illogical. Make sure you understand how people perceive it and understand you.

- Be careful that the pain you are willing to take as you sacrifice and suffer for your vision doesn't make you inflexible or blind you to necessary adjustments and course corrections.

- Discovering your true passion and then driving forward with energy and excitement are huge parts of your success in execution. Those emotions make it possible to put in the work in action, and they give you the power to endure when you need resilience. Sharing your passion binds you to others in relationships.

BEFORE YOU GO: WHAT'S THE SCENARIO?

This scenario is designed to help you think about everything you have learned in this section. Please take a few minutes to complete this exercise as best you can. I promise it will be worth it. If you get stuck or you are not sure about your answer, go back and review the section. Remember, there is no right or wrong answer here. This is just a way of applying your new knowledge about passion.

Often it is easier to give advice to someone else, when you're not wrapped up in your own world, full of all its complexities. A friend has always enjoyed her job. She likes what she does and the people she does it with, and has always felt challenged. However, lately she has been feeling bored and disengaged, and her work and health are suffering.

How would you use the concepts you've learned about passion to help her?

ACTION

Taking That First Step and the Next One

A journey of a thousand miles
begins with a single step.
—LAO TZU

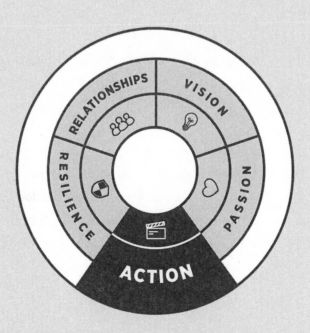

10

Setting the Stage to Act

"Kim, are you ready?" the producers asked me.

What did they mean? Was I ready for the 10-day trip to Tel Aviv and then Germany I was supposed to take in the morning? Or was I ready for my first public speech on execution I was supposed to give to 2,000 people in less than two hours at this beautiful event? An event where I was on the bill with acclaimed speakers whose work I greatly admired? They were authors and accomplished veterans of the stage. I was the new kid on the block, and the conversation quickly shifted focus to my talk.

"So, Kim, how many times have you given this speech on execution?"

"Never."

"No, no, sorry. We meant how many times have you given this speech *generally*, not the specific one you're giving for our event?"

"Nope, still never."

"Wait, you've *never* given this talk before?"

"Nope. Aside from trying an early version out on a few of my employees, I've never spoken to any audience on execution before."

"Are you kidding?" they laughed nervously.

I shook my head no.

"Seriously?"

I smiled. I could see some of them who were involved in the planning of the event turning a little white, concerned they had even invited me. Sensing that concern and worrying that whatever I said next might get someone fired, I decided not to add that I had never even spoken to an audience this large on any topic.

Because in actuality, none of that mattered for me taking the stage for the first time to talk about execution. I knew I could be successful. I pushed their reactions to the side.

"Kim, are you ready?"

Of course I was! I wasn't just ready. I was prepared to lead with action. When given a chance to seize an opportunity to take the first step or the next step to realizing my vision, I take it. I always take it.

Take That First Step

The question I get asked most often by entrepreneurs is: "I have a great idea. Where do I start?" The answer is, *"Take the first step!"* In most instances, the first step is so easy: Just do. Dive in. Motion creates motion. Just *go*. And trust me, I understand taking the first step is often the hardest part in an entrepreneur's journey. But there's no magic formula for success, and you don't need 100 percent certainty or even have to know the ultimate destination. You just have to move forward.

I asked some of the most successful executives and entrepreneurs if where they are today is where they thought they would be when they started out in business. None of them said yes. You know I didn't. My dot-com career went down in flames as quickly as it started. I had no choice but to act. The question was, what choice would I make to act on? I chose Hawaii and starting my own company. The problem is that's what too many people with brilliant ideas *don't* do. They get stuck in analysis paralysis and come up with every reason why not to take the plunge: from finances to the team to the business plan being "not quite right." Unless you would be doing something illegal or unless lives or the well-being of others would be at stake, these are just excuses for shying away from the first step.

People can't believe I can block out all the noise and act. But that's what you must do to take the first step and act. I've seen this happen dozens of times in my digital career. Two companies have similar ideas: One spends all its time planning and strategizing; the other goes and attempts to build toward its vision. In the end, the company that took action may not have built the better product, but it *acted* and made it to market first. Sure, that company hit a few dips before becoming successful, but most companies— like people—rarely achieve success exactly they way they planned it. Success is not linear. It's the same messy line to the top.

That said, I do not recommend that first step be quitting your day job. I've seen that happen all too often. If your bank account is empty, then you shouldn't quit what is making you money. My grandfather always said, "Make hay when the sun is shining." If you have a family, it's even more important: family first! Remember my cautionary tale about my father: don't go all in on the next thing or the side hustle until you absolutely have to. Keep it as a side hustle until you can clearly see that you can live off the profits it makes, get funding, or secure a loan to make sure it pays your bills.

I didn't quit my job as a CEO to pursue my passion for execution after I nailed it on that stage that day. *But* Stacey did. She was a health and wellness nut who worked in corporate finance and wanted to start her own juicing company. She took the right first steps and started working weekends at a farmers' market, developing devoted juice fans. That's when she decided to leave her well-paying job to start her own juice company. But she went all in on juice without having a clear business plan to ensure that she could pay the bills. Eventually, she ran out of savings and had to go find a new job.

Acting on a vision doesn't mean all or nothing. It's truly about trial and error and course corrections, learning what you don't know so you can act with more and more certainty. But even then you may never be certain! And that's OK. It's impossible to predict what will happen. You can always change. Just move. Start. Start now!

However, when you do act, don't expect that first step to keep you growing and executing at the highest levels. More than the "Beware!" of acting with total uncertainty or a complete lack of planning, if your action doesn't evolve to the next step—if you get stuck repeating the first step over and over, competition and imitation come calling quickly in the digital age. One need only think about Apple to understand what I mean. Apple wasn't first to market with its MP3 player or smartphone. It didn't invent voice activation or facial recognition. It simply evolved the technology faster and then marketed it better than its competition.

That's a key lesson in action. Apple acted and kept acting to reaffirm the passion (meaning emotional connection) people had to its brand—even when other brands produced products that equaled or bettered Apple's. That's how they were able to stay on top and become one of the most iconic and valuable brands in the world. A brand that people are unquestionably loyal to. Because it's never just about the product. People act on passion. Apple is not selling iPhones. McDonald's is not selling hamburgers. Google is not selling searches. Nike is not selling sneakers. Amazon is not selling products. They are selling you visions of a better, more connected, and more convenient life to make you want something and act. You need to remember this as you act. In fact, if I hadn't acted on my passion, my career and life would have looked vastly different.

Your First Step Is What You Make It

Clearly, there are some situations in which there are very serious and far-reaching consequences that require more planning and thought than other situations do when it comes to executing your vision. Big change and big actions often generate big resistance in others and in you. But more often than not, big is what you make it in your mind, and that big feeling prevents you from taking that first step. You might think that the first step for me was getting on that plane to Hawaii to start my first business. Yet I might never have had the courage to get on that plane if I hadn't acted in a smaller way first.

When I was a freshman in college, I had a serious crush on this guy in my math class. Before we went into the classroom, I sat outside and listened to him tell stories of growing up and surfing in Hawaii. I'd never been to Hawaii, but it sounded so cool and exotic to me, a girl from Portland, Oregon. I wished he would ask me out. He didn't. Instead, after listening for weeks every day before class, I committed to myself to make the first move. I went to his dorm room one night and asked him out on a date. Sure, it wasn't exactly common for girls to ask the boys out on my campus, and there was a chance he would say no. But what if he said *yes*?! Any risk of rejection outweighed the potential outcome of the date, so I pushed rejection out of my mind, and I turned a deaf ear to my friends who told me I was crazy or that I should "wait for him to ask me." I walked to his dorm, and knocked with confidence.

Fast-forward 20 years later and we're married and teaching our twins how to surf. And it all started with me resolving to push past any excuses and resistance and acting by

- Taking the first step.
- Prioritizing the action.
- Acting even though it was uncomfortable.
- Taking the next step and then the next and the next . . .

What was the worst thing that could have happened when I asked my future husband out? He could have said no? My friends made potential rejection such a *big* deal. It wasn't— rejection never is. It would just have been a different first step to realizing my vision of our being together. The stakes were not as high as people made them out to be. Most of the time a first step is neither an end nor irreversible. Some don't even have major consequences. We just agonize over rejection instead of finding another path to a path.

· · · · · · · · · · · ·

One step is all you need to get going.

· · · · · · · · · · · ·

Whether it is love or business or anywhere in between, too many of us spend too much time worrying about the possible failure or rejection and the obstacles that could get in our way. We can't live in the realm of "maybe" or "what if." That can be paralyzing. A little healthy skepticism is natural, but the reality is that most of the time the worst thing you think could happen won't. Don't worry about what will happen in a week, a month, or a year. Just *act*! Your first inclination should be to *do* something—anything—to get you moving in the right direction, no matter how small that step may be. Go forth and start conquering!

The Japanese have a word for this in business and life: *kaizen*. Basically, *kaizen* is about making continuous positive changes to increase productivity and improve your life. Each step may seem small, but taken cumulatively, what they lead to is big change. My small step to ask a guy out in college promised nothing more than the sting of rejection as a negative consequence. But that same small step led not only to my marriage but to the opportunity to move with him to Hawaii, start my first business, and execute my vision of freedom, being my own boss, and controlling my destiny.

Sure, there were many other steps that followed. But when I asked my husband out, I stopped doing what normally gets in the way of small first steps: procrastinating.

So:

- How do you take that first step—and the next one—and prioritize, not procrastinate?
- How will you keep your actions aligned with your vision and passion?
- How can you manage resistance, doubt, fear, uncertainty, and risk and keep acting?

Let's explore all of these questions further and get into *action*.

ACTION CHECK

Questions for Self-Reflection

People who lead with action seize the day for the right opportunity to make things happen. Think about a time you seized the day and acted.

What was your first step?

What happened?

How did it make you feel?

What was the result?

Prioritize Action: Better to Start Than Procrastinate

D espite my entrepreneurial DNA, I admit I used to think the actions that lead to success followed a fairly straight line to the top. Naive, right? As a teenager and college grad, I believed a successful life was going to be simple: I would go to college, get a job, and start a family—each a step up on that straight line to success. This turned out to be far from reality. But that's okay because success would have been only a fraction as fulfilling as it has been if the path had been linear. Success required me to constantly seize every opportunity to take first steps forward and then the next one, no matter how unpleasant they were.

Back before I knew success was that messy line to the top, one of my mentors asked me why I saw everything as a step-by-step progression. "Could you see it and do it on parallel paths?" he asked. I never looked at action the same way again.

Prioritizing your vision is connected to prioritizing the actions that directly relate to executing that vision. That correlation is why I keep my vision posted at the top of my to-do list to make sure the things at the top of my list are connected to it. Unfortunately, too many of us never even get to our to-do lists. A lot of research has been done with college students, and the data shows that as many as 70 percent of them procrastinate. *While that number drops after college, up to 25 percent of people admit to significant procrastination as adults.*[1]

Some researchers have divided these procrastinators into types. The first is the "arousal" procrastinator: *Arousal procrastinators* are people who need the rush of adrenaline created by urgency to execute and thus wait to the last minute. The second type of procrastinator is more dangerous to execution: the "avoidant" procrastinator.[2]

Avoidant procrastinators can't engage in the task. This is often because they don't think they have the ability to do it or that it simply does not inspire them to action. I'll address doubting your ability or lack of inspiration shortly. But there is another big reason that gets in the way of taking that first step and all the other steps going on around you. You have reasons for *not* acting:

> I have to do this for my boss.
> My client needs this now.
> My kid needs a ride.
> I'm hungry.
> I can't afford it right now.
> I'm tired.

Every one of those reasons may be true, important, and even urgent. But one thing is for sure: reasons *do not* motivate us to act on our vision. They only lead to *answers*—usually reasons why not. That is, *excuses*. Remember: Passion is about suffering for vision—no excuses.

Action is about prioritizing that first step and the next so you hold yourself accountable—no excuses! Even if it means working late when you're tired and you would rather be in bed watching your favorite TV show. It's of course much harder to do that when someone else—be it your boss, client, or family—is holding you accountable for your actions (or "nonactions"), but there are plenty of hours left in the day when no one is holding you accountable but *you*. But you must. Undoubtedly, this can be hard to do when so many different things are pulling you in different directions. I get it, but you have to prioritize and persevere.

If You Keep Doing What Is Comfortable and Easiest, You'll Get Stuck

Most people don't procrastinate enjoyable activities, like going on a vacation. We procrastinate when we are faced with uncertainty or actions that we believe will in some way be unpleasant or have unknown outcomes. We procrastinate delivering bad news or doing something difficult because the easiest actions give us the satisfaction of getting something done. But let's recall the words of President John F. Kennedy, whose vision to reach the moon kicked off the work on these traits of execution: "There are risks and costs to a program of action. But they are far less than the long-range risks and costs of comfortable inaction."

Think about your procrastination. It probably occurs when you have to take actions you don't want to take or you are unsure about, or they are outside of your comfort zone. In most cases, putting it off only makes the situation worse and makes the first step even harder because you're thinking about it too much!

Action Pulse Check

Think about the last time you had to deliver bad news. What happened when you finally delivered it?

Now take some hard-to-deliver news (no matter how small it is) and deliver it. Find the right place to do it— preferably in person but if not, on the phone and if necessary by e-mail (not text). Take note of how you feel afterward.

Stop just checking boxes on your to-do list, and instead *do the hardest thing first no matter how unpleasant it might be*. I'm not against doing certain tasks because you love doing them, but it usually means you are putting off doing something more difficult. *No one ever failed to achieve their goals because they did the harder thing first instead of laundry*. I prioritized my vision and passion and created the opportunity by doing difficult, even intimidating, things. I gave them quality time and a higher emotional value, and I was willing to suffer for them. Then, I acted and persisted no matter how hard or unpleasant the actions were.

People have never achieved their goals
and reached their visions because
they did the easiest things first.

I remember as a teenager my grandfather wanted my sister, brother, and me to read a new Rush Limbaugh book. We all loved our grandfather, but that wasn't going to happen. It wasn't about Rush's politics. It was because his book was 300 pages long, and we had better things to do, including nothing at all. As a teenager, "nothing" was better than the unpleasantness of reading that book.

Then I had a vision that made my grandfather's vision mine. I told him if he paid me to read it, I would write him a summary. I ended up making $20. I had just found a way to make it a priority and take the first step.

Every journey starts with that first page—that first step to your goal:

- If you want to be a chef, take a cooking class.
- If you want to be an artist, take an art class.
- If you want to start a business, go do the research.
- If you want to write a book, write the first sentence.
- If you want your grandfather to pay you to read a book, make a deal.

And what's after that first step? Your *next* step—and every step after that! I cannot emphasize this enough: It's *really* easy to get stuck in an action by getting too comfortable with any step in the process. The goal is to keep moving forward and making progress to the goal or finish line. Do not repeat the same step over again because that gets boring!

You probably have heard some version of this line before: the definition of *insanity* is doing the same thing over and over and expecting a different result. In action, the definition of *insanity* is doing the same thing over and over and expecting to move forward. Think of it this way: it is entirely possible to run 26.2 miles—the length of a marathon—by running 1 mile, turning around, running back to the start, and then running the first mile again about nine times. You cover the same distance and use up just as much energy as the regular marathon without ever advancing past the first mile.

The Next Steps to Realizing Your Vision

Executing in business is all about growth. But doing the same thing over and over only leads to managing the growth you have, not evolving to create new steps to act and opportunities to grow and execute your vision.

Even I have made this mistake. While no one has ever said to me, "Kim, you need to act!" about something I cared about, I have missed some next steps. Not because I repeated steps or hesitated or thought the action was too risky but because I didn't go far enough, see the need to scale in my next steps, or failed to put more money in. Other times, I acted and realized too late that I didn't understand the whole picture when I thought I had planned everything out.

A couple of times that actually caused my entire company pain—actual pain.

As a team bonding experience, I decided a great exercise to help people "break through" their fears and increase their confidence would be breaking wooden boards karate style. None of us knew karate, but we were told in the instructions we read that five-year-olds could push through one of the boards. How much fun would this be?

Everyone was into it. "You can do it!" we all screamed as employee after employee approached the boards, brought their hands crashing down, and . . . failed to break a single board.

No one could do it.

This exercise was supposed to be about confidence, not contusions. Yet that's what everyone was getting as they failed to break the board and grabbed their hands in pain. Turned out we had the boards cut the wrong way. You apparently have to have the wood cut with the grain for this to work. We didn't. We were trying to break boards for bonding, but we had failed to read that part of the instructions, let alone specify the right way to cut the boards at Home Depot!

To avoid breaking more bones in the future, I have learned that next steps often require more planning and focus than you think—a more holistic vision to ensure that you have identified the path to your vision and know what you don't know. You must understand this too:

Six Things You Should Do Before You Act

1. Identify additional action steps.
2. Create a time frame.
3. Build in accountability.
4. Anticipate possible obstacles.
5. Create a list of resources.
6. Create a review process.

1. Identify Additional Action Steps

Identify the steps that will enable you to realize your vision. Then plan out your steps in sequence, knowing that the next step is the most important and that subsequent steps might change as your journey evolves.

Be ready and open to pivot when you need to. That way you won't miss the opportunities right in front of you and those that offer the next opportunities.

2. Create a Time Frame

Set realistic time frames for completing the next step and subsequent steps.

The balance here is in creating time frames that give you enough time to make it happen—but also put enough pressure on you to get going. Too far out and it might be hard to get started; too close and it might feel like too much pressure.

3. Build in Accountability

Ensure that steps are completed. Commit to someone or something.

Is it a friend, a colleague, boss? Whatever you do, make sure you have some measures for accountability to encourage you to stay on track.

4. Anticipate Possible Obstacles

How might you overcome obstacles and anticipate what you don't know? Think about what might get in the way or stop you.

Don't dwell on this, but at least consider what the obstacles might be and how you will deal with them should they arise.

5. Create a List of Resources

Be specific on what you will need to execute—and don't lowball! My grandfather taught me this rule when I was young, and I think about it all the time. Everything will be twice as hard, take twice as long, and cost twice as much as you think it will.

Consider everything you're going to need for effective action, and make the next step happen. Do you need money, and if so, how much? Do you need people, and if so, what are their skills or respective roles? Do you need equipment, and if so, where can you get it?

6. Create a Review Process

You need to review to keep properly focused on progress. Every action is a potential lesson that can inform you about your business. Record your actions and the results, and make sure you measure what you do and how it turns out.

People who lead with action will find taking these steps frustrating—we'd rather just *do*. But we must review. Take a few minutes to think about them, and answer those questions. As with all of the traits, there is a caution for those who lead with action: the willingness to step in and take on a challenge may have gotten you where you are today, but it also can be your downfall, if it leads you away from your vision and isolates you from others.

ACTION CHECK

Questions for Self-Reflection

There's no substitute for taking action. Anything else is just an excuse.

What actions will you take?

What are your first and next steps?

How will you prioritize them?

How have you let excuses and fear of rejection stop you in the past? How can you get past that in the future?

12

Vision Quest

When I was three, I wanted to lie in a hammock. We didn't have a hammock, and my parents were not going to buy me a hammock. So I strung a sheet up between two doors in our house and made myself a hammock. I remember hitting the ground hard in my first attempt to secure the sheets to the knobs. This became my earliest evidence of living one of my mottos: "Fail fast, learn, and move on." On my second try, I succeeded and fell comfortably asleep in my hammock until my parents woke me up for dinner.

When I was five, I wanted a pool, but we didn't have the money to build one. The Portland, Oregon, weather didn't justify it. My first attempt that spring to build one did not please my parents as much as the hammock had: I locked the bathroom door, wedged a towel under the crack at the bottom, and filled the entire room with dish soap and water. I was enjoying my bubble pool until my parents arrived home to soapy water gushing through the roof of the dining room. My second try was more successful that summer: I took all the sand out of my sandbox and put a green tarp down and filled it with water to make the pool of my dreams. I spent countless days that summer playing in it.

When I was eight, my desires had become more manageable but couldn't be solved by creatively using what we had around the house: I wanted a comic book. My parents told me if I wanted it, I needed to find a way to earn it. That's when I learned you get 5 cents for returning a can to the supermarket in Oregon. Money did not grow on trees, but it did lie in trash bins! Every can I saw in a bin or in people's hands as they drank looked like opportunity. I pulled my red wagon from door to door in my neighborhood collecting the cans. Neighbors soon started saving them for me, and it added up fast.

So when I say my actions have always been in line with my visions to get what I wanted—even the small ones like those I just described and eventually those horseback riding lessons I bartered for at 11—I pretty much mean always.

But as a teenager my visions went beyond hammocks and horses. In high school, my vision for my "life" got much bigger: owning a red Jeep Wrangler.

I had a clear, compelling vision of this Jeep. I loved the feeling of freedom it would give me as I thought about it. I could feel myself driving down the road, wind in my hair, top down, 1990s music blasting. I pictured myself driving it to school and picking up my friends and talking about our days. We would go to the river and listen to Bon Jovi.

I *had* to have that Jeep, and it had to be *red*. I was determined. I taped up pictures of that Jeep in my room and got to work. First, I made a deal with my dad and mom: they agreed to match every dollar I earned to buy the Jeep. No after-school sports or activities for me. I worked any job I could find. I folded sweaters and ran the cash register at a clothing store. I made pizza. I sold men's suits. I worked at a candy store. I babysat. I was focused and willing to do whatever it took to get that Jeep. I even built in accountability by having my dad regularly check in on whether I was reaching my savings target.

And I did it. It took me two years from the time I had the vision, but I finally got the money to put a down payment on the Jeep. But most importantly, it was the first time I understood the power of having my goal visible so I could see it and revisit it over and over again. While other people at work were moaning and complaining, I generally had a smile on my face because I knew I would soon be driving my red Jeep. Everything I was doing was directly connected to my vision taped up in my room. I had purpose, focus, and accountability to my vision. I had to continue to work to pay for the monthly payments, but I didn't care. I knew going in that was part of the deal with my dad, and I was prepared to do whatever it took to get it and keep it.

Congratulations, you're halfway through our journey through execution! Time to reflect back on vision and make sure you have this too.

Don't Mistake Busyness for Progress

In a world of limited time and resources, you need to carefully choose where to invest your energy and actions. Be selective. *What is important along every step of the way is that your actions are aligned with your vision and your passion for it.* That way you always ensure that those actions aren't just checkmarks on a to-do list—or worse, checkmarks on a to-do list for the visions others told you to pursue.

This is why you must create that constant daily review process for your actions and make sure your actions align with your vision, not just the bottom line:

- Is where you are going still where you want to go?
- Are your actions helping you achieve your vision and fostering your passion?

Think back to the scenario in Chapter 3 and Darren whose friends and family told him he made the best chili in the entire world and convinced him to quit his job and open a food truck. He was miserable. What happened? He took the first step. He even took some of the next steps and planned well. But Darren never wanted to open a food truck: the food truck was *their vision for him.* How did he think pursuing their vision could last when he never saw it for himself?

· · · · · · · · · · · ·

Without vision, action is just busyness.
Without passion, it's boring.

· · · · · · · · · · · ·

Sometimes it is easy to check the alignment between your actions and your vision and passion. When I got on that plane to Hawaii to start my first business with only the money I had borrowed from my grandmother, I remember asking myself, "Am I crazy?" But I quickly remembered my goals for my vision that I had written down long before I left: freedom, to be my own boss, and to control my destiny. The delete button had been pushed on my professional identity, my income, and my future, and I had vowed *never* to let that happen again.

It's when the steps start adding up and speeding up that you need to check yourself. Really think about what it is that you want and are working toward. After all, it is your vision and passion that keep you going when the actions inevitably get to be a real slog. As Yogi Berra said, "If you don't know where you're going, you might not get there":

- *Visions can evolve.* Is yours still where you started?
- *Passions can wane.* Are you still willing to suffer for your vision?

Only when the answer to these questions is yes can you have progress—both for yourself and others.

Consider another version of the food truck scenario from the vision section: What if Darren *did* have a vision to open a food truck, but he didn't love cooking food for anyone but his closest friends and family? His execution would dissipate because he wasn't pursuing his passion. But gut checks are not always this easy and clear before the first step.

For example, what if Darren did love serving chili to all people and making them happy? He could picture himself in the truck. Sure, he knew it was a tough business, but he loved chili and loved making it. Then he discovered that there were already *two* popular chili food trucks in town. Competition for the chili dollars was fierce, but the food truck scene was hot. So Darren pivoted. He researched what kind of food trucks were missing in town and one stood out: Chinese food.

There was only one problem: Darren hated Chinese food, never made it, and never ate it. But the demand was there, so he pursued that path, eventually quit his job, and opened the truck. Six months later, he found himself making money, but he was stressed and angry. The truck was doing fine, but he was not. He mismanaged his expectations. When he got an offer to sell it at a breakeven price, he jumped at it and immediately returned to his old job.

What happened? This time Darren took steps toward his vision of a food truck, and it was his passion, right? So why did he fail? Because *he was suffering for only part of his passion.* Despite his vision and passion for the food truck scene, he had no emotional connection to the single thing he would be connected to: the food. Even though he was successful, he came into work every day hating the product he produced.

Sometimes this matters, especially when you are personally connected to the product, not just the process. I never cared what jobs I had as long as I earned money toward my pursuit of my red Jeep. I wasn't producing what I sold. Same thing when it came to not worrying about what I sold once we set up my first business in Hawaii. I sold toy cars, teeth whiteners, doggie sunglasses . . . whatever it took to get me to where I wanted to be. My passion was for the process, not the product. But if your passion is connected to the product and the process, then you can't let either be out of alignment.

And without that alignment between vision, passion, and action, you'll never inspire others to join you and act on your behalf to scale the vision you have.

Action Pulse Check

Do what Darren failed to do when he executed his vision for opening a food truck. Break your passion down into two parts: *process* and *product*. For him that was running a business cooking and serving others (process) and chili (product).

Do you have passion for both sides of the list, and are they aligned with your actions? If not, adjust your passion and actions—or consider whether your vision is not what you actually want to act on.

Action Without Others Is Lonely

I love what I do. I also love just as much that I get to work with some of the most talented individuals in my industry. I've worked with some of the same people for nearly 20 years, but I'm prouder to call them my friends. In fact, my office is right next to the office of my best friend from college. That's why every time I see someone acting alone, I always feel a tinge of sadness—regardless of whether I disagree or agree with the action.

You need others to help you take the
next steps and develop a culture of action in
which to scale your vision and grow.

Getting people to act on your vision in business does not need to be a lonely experience, nor should it be. Other people give you different perspectives on your action based on their personal experiences. They give you peripheral vision and feedback, and they prepare you for potential blind spots. We'll cover this in depth in Trait 5, "Relationships," but when it comes to action, know that as you grow, you need to bring people in and surround yourself with others who want to help you act.

There are so many different and new opportunities that if you look at them from only one perspective, you may miss opportunities. I need people who can see them too. It is important not just to do what you are told—or focus exclusively on the risks and downsides.

As you have probably guessed, repetitive action is not my style. I am always looking to take the next step. Yet unlike running a marathon, you can't always leave the first steps behind. You need to hire help or automate actions that are repeatable and not the best use of your time so you can move on to the next steps. That means not only delegating to others those actions that have become systematic (even the ones you love to do) but also empowering other people to take actions.

Allow your people to take action and push forward in ways you might not see or have considered—as long as what they do aligns with the company vision.

I've been the CEO of businesses with hundreds of employees, and I still call myself an entrepreneur—someone who feels like she's just starting, pushing boundaries, willing to take risks to grow. I want anyone who works for me or with me to feel the same way. Bottom to top, I don't want anyone confined to a box—people can't just do what they're told. So I'm naturally more hands-off than some executives, and I expect my leaders to be the same way. I also don't want the people I surround myself with to act like me. I *want them* to challenge and push me and themselves forward. I do not want a table full of naysayers. I do want people to play devil's advocates. I'm happy to have a bunch of entrepreneurs acting entrepreneurial in the service of achieving the goals of the company.

How can we do that? By creating autonomous work environments that allow your employees to be "intrapreneurs." Intrapreneurs are entrepreneurs within the walls of the company they work for. They get job security, but they also have the opportunity to work as individuals in identifying, anticipating, and pursuing opportunities.

How do you create that? Just let it happen. Don't try to make people conform to one vantage point because conformity will get you only one way—and not necessarily the best way—of doing things. Allow people to teach you and create, innovate, and imagine any idea possible. Allow them to be individuals and express their individuality. We can still be a team serving the goals of the company or our vision *and* demand results *and* have individuality. It's wrong to think that those actions have to be in conflict. In fact, working in that type of environment is how your employees and coworkers will learn to challenge you and most importantly themselves. You don't win by having people focus on mitigating the risk of their actions. You don't succeed by just following the safe choices.

And you can't always rely on what the data tells you at first glance. We all want the comfort of certainty. Numbers can provide that comfort. But even numbers can be an illusion. In a quest to feel more comfortable about our decisions, we can use data to engage in seeking confirmation bias, which works this way: having made a decision, we seek out all the data that confirms our judgment and we ignore all the data that disagrees with it. We get the illusion of certainty through selective attention. That's not a good idea. Better to let the data tell all its stories.

I was watching the movie *Hidden Figures*, a dramatization of the untold story of African-American women who worked as mathematicians or human "calculators" for NASA at the start of the space race. The United States had fallen behind Russia and meeting President Kennedy's challenge to reach the moon by the end of the decade. In one scene, Katherine Johnson (who was a real-life hero and, at 97 years old, received the Presidential Medal of Freedom from President Barack Obama) is pressed by her supervisor about how she came up with the correct calculations for a rocket launch despite all the redacted information in the document.

"Well, what's there tells a story if you read between the lines," she says. She did the math, she said, and "looked beyond" the data.

It's indisputable that Katherine Johnson and the other female African-American mathematicians disrupted the culture of NASA and forced the men to see problems and people differently. They were instrumental in helping the United States reclaim the momentum from the Russians and reach the moon first. While the world outside pushed people of color to the margins of society, NASA knew that a culture of action is no good if it doesn't challenge and disrupt, allowing people to "look beyond":

- You need to encourage disruption—different ideas or ways of doing things—in the workplace and marketplace and support it with your actions.

- You need a strong organization and leadership to do this to mitigate the chaos of a lot of parallel actions and explorations, not to mention the risks.
- Your people need to be held accountable for their actions, but they do not, and in some cases should not, follow the same next steps you take.

But some words of warning as you look beyond: *People who lead with action have to remember that not everyone does.* Take a moment and remember that you may want to *go go go*, but others who lead with one of the other traits may act slower, and speed is not always the fastest path to success for everyone.

It *Is* a Journey

People who don't know me are often surprised how much I value the idea that the journey itself is the destination. Part of this comes from my parents, intrepid entrepreneurs who drove around the country looking for places to live. It was a latent bit of DNA, I admit. I used to think the destination was the destination, just as I used to think success was a linear progression. The willingness to take on any challenge has gotten me to where I am today, but I would get lost if I focused only on the action—and thus lost not only perspective but also the joy of the journey.

Your journey should be enjoyable
and, yes, fun.

And it is *all* a journey! Let me tell you something about work-life balance: It is illusive and elusive.

It's not as much about a work-life separation or balance as it is about a work-life integration.

The distinction between work and play is actually arbitrary, a function of the binary brain that likes to divide the world into polar opposites. Often work feels like play, and sometimes play feeds your work. I have had some of my best ideas when vacationing! Why not share them? Technology has enabled us to be available 24/7. Resistance may not be futile, but what are you fighting? And how much is it costing you? This is why I don't mind taking a conference call on vacation—because the reality is that I'm able to enjoy my vacation more by doing this.

My success is defined by doing what I love with people I care about every day and helping them achieve their visions. Success is best when shared—with employees, partners, clients, friends, family, and your community. So I try to create and maintain as many synergies as possible within all areas of my life. That does not stop me from doing what I love—in fact, it has allowed me to do more of what I love as I have taken each step forward.

For example, I love to travel. Working for a global company, I not only get to travel for work but I can also have my husband fly out for a four-day weekend to explore Paris, Tokyo, or Berlin. Because my visions, passions, and actions infuse each other, I never feel like I am missing anything because I refuse to accept that they *must* be separated in order to have balance. When you act, you must maintain the important relationships in your life so you never feel totally alone, even in the most stressful times. If you don't, your actions might still lead to success, but the only one celebrating and toasting you will be . . . you.

Questions for Self-Reflection

On a scale from 1 to 10, how are your current actions directly related to your vision?

On a scale from 1 to 10, how are your current actions fostering your passion?

On a scale from 1 to 10, how are your current actions bringing you joy and connecting you to those you care about?

If your answers are low or you feel a sense of stress or doubt when you act, take some time to assess why. Double-check that it's what is right for you and what you want. You may need to go back to your vision and make sure it is what you truly desire and are passionate about before moving forward. Often, our visions are things others want or expect from us, but those visions aren't what we truly desire or they are driving us away from the people we care about most.

13

Fear of Flying

O nyema lived in a poor Nigerian village with her grandmother because her mother had to work in a neighboring village. When she was six, she saw a plane flying overhead for the first time, and was so awestruck that as she soon as she discovered what it was, she vowed to be a pilot. This seemed impossible to those around her.

Onyema refused to give in to the seeming impossibility of her vision. Her passion drove her to keep going and do well in school in addition to all the other work she had to do in the village. When she was the equivalent of a high school senior, she took a 12-hour bus ride to the capital and found an Internet café where she planned to apply to the University of Alabama for a place in its aerospace course. However, the application cost money, and she didn't have any. That's when some locals, hearing her story, gave her the money for her application. Onyema was soon accepted.

The following school year, Onyema left her village and flew to Atlanta. When she got to Atlanta, she had a new problem: she hadn't realized she needed another flight to Tuscaloosa, and she again didn't have the funds to pay for her flight. So she found a local Nigerian couple in Atlanta who were willing to help. They gave her a place to stay for the night and later made church collections for her tuition and even gave her a car. Onyema made it to the University of Alabama that fall, but even with the help she had been given, she couldn't afford to stay the full four years. In the end, she attended several schools, often doing one semester at a time because she didn't have the funds to pay for a full year's tuition.

Today Onyema is an aerospace engineer and has started a charity to encourage African women to explore STEM studies. She has spoken alongside the Nigerian minister for education and other senior officials in her home country.

Onyema's story is beyond inspiring. She is the perfect example of the importance of taking it one step at a time and using your passion to push through to achieve your vision. Can you imagine the fear and doubt she had to overcome to execute her vision, especially one that seemed so far-fetched to everyone she had grown up with?

Sometimes you know your vision, feel deeply connected to your passion, devise an action plan designed to accomplish your goals, write each step down, assign a timeline, ensure that accountability is built in, and . . . still don't manage to take action. We've all been there before: when fear and doubt get in the way of action and making decisions that lead to successful execution.

Hey, the actions you take can be life changing, and the prospect of executing something big and far-reaching can be daunting. It's okay to be afraid that you will fail just as it is okay to fail fast, learn, and move on.

Onyema has been there. I've been there, but like us, you cannot let fear stop you from acting and executing.

Successful Executors
Feel the Fear and *Act Anyway*

While Onyema's dream was to be a pilot, I'm the opposite. I have an enormous fear of flying. Whenever I'm on a plane, I'm overcome with palm-sweating, white-knuckle fear. But that doesn't stop me from getting on a plane nearly every week and traveling the world for both business and pleasure. Yes, statistically I know I am more likely to die from a car crash then a plane crash, but fear isn't necessarily rational.

I just never let my fear—or any fears, doubts, or other obstacles—stop me from taking action to achieve my goals, and I am not going to start by refusing to get on a plane.

The fact is that human beings, like other animals, were originally designed to survive by avoiding dangerous situations. Our brains are wired to look for "the negative" and avoid it. That's why even in business today, if we sense a threat—something that makes us scared, something risky, or even just something uncomfortable—we become overcautious because we think our survival depends on it. So we play it safe. We make comfortable choices even though most of us know the magic happens when we get out of our comfort zones.

Simply put, we overvalue fear. As a result, we can easily get carried away with our worst fears and let them influence our thoughts and actions.

This is why we must learn to manage our emotions so that we recognize and acknowledge them but don't overvalue them and give them too much power. But this also means we need to develop a mindset that is an antidote to fear and stress. This is where keeping constantly connected to your vision is so critical.

It will help protect you from being overwhelmed by stress, from overvaluing it and allowing it to change your thought process. Moreover, passion and motivation are connected in the brain and are mediated by the same neurotransmitter: dopamine. You can think of dopamine as the high-grade fuel needed for the long journey ahead.

Instead of feeling the fear, taking it in, and turning it into action to power us through, most of us let fear overwhelm us instead. I refuse to let fear overinfluence me, and so must you. If I did, I wouldn't get out of bed. I'd pull up the sheets and hide.

> Don't let fear, doubt, or uncertainty
> stop you from taking action.

I have learned to deal with my fears—embrace and manage them as I execute, and so must you. Resolve to control them and not let them control you. Remember: Emotional mastery is essential to successful action because we feel emotions only in the present. Your worst fears are not certainties, just overvalued anxieties. They are connected to the present, not the future. Fear can prevent us from taking the next step. It is about how you feel you are going to feel. Anticipation of a plane crash is not forecasting a crash. It is about how you feel getting on that plane. You are feeling the worry about it *now*, not what will happen—any facts you are dealing with are actually just probabilities, not certainties.

Negative feelings—or even positive ones like love and trust—can distort everything with extreme lows and highs. Don't let them overwhelm you. Take them in and master them. That goes for doubt too.

Don't Doubt Yourself

Doubt is trickier than fear to master because it sounds much more rational. And that's exactly what it is, a rationalization:

> The time is not right.
> I don't have all the information I need.
> It's going to take a lot of effort.
> I don't know whether I will succeed.

Those are just some of the ways doubt gives you permission to play it safe or not take action. To avoid getting trapped, the first step is to stop measuring everything by success or failure. No one wins all the time. Only the best hitters in baseball bat more than .333, which means few get a hit in more than one-third of those at bats. The biggest home run hitters usually bat much lower. The last one to hit more than .400 was Ted Williams in 1941. The point isn't how often you fail or succeed but that when given the most important opportunities to act, you execute and take another step toward success.

So here's my question for you: Are you ready to take that step?

That's a trick question. Of course, you're ready! If you are in action, then you're ready:

- Don't wait. Push aside your fears. Trust yourself and your instincts.
- Don't think you have to start small or even big. Everyone has to start somewhere.
- Don't wait for the perfect conditions. Conditions and timing will never be perfect. *It's about progress before perfection.*

This is where keeping constantly connected to your vision is so critical. As we covered in the section on passion, emotions are essential to executing our visions because they drive the stories we tell ourselves and seriously influence our thoughts and thus actions. Most of the time these thoughts are driven by the need for emotional comfort and consistency. This means in times of stress, we will distort the narrative, often leading to an unwarranted change of direction—a step away from what we fear or doubt will work.

Remember: Successful executors take action. They know there is no wrong first step. The same grandfather who told me to make hay when the sun is shining also told me, "A path leads to a path," and I have almost always found that to be true. Even if that path leads me to what won't work, I'm still a step closer to what will. Acting with total uncertainty or complete lack of planning is very different from not trusting yourself.

I have learned not to doubt myself or hesitate when faced with a degree of risk and uncertainty, especially if the action is deeply aligned with my vision and passion. That means I'm willing to suffer for it, which is what I was doing the day I delivered my first speech on execution. I gave up my family time, refused to let the 10-day work trip that started the next day be an excuse for not accepting the invitation, and got on a plane (which, as you now know, I hate). And while I might have checked in with myself before I went on stage, I never doubted that my actions would deliver. You don't fake it 'til you make it. You do it and make it real! I refused to worry about aiming too much before I fired.

· · · · · · · · · · ·

Progress before perfection.

· · · · · · · · · · ·

Actually, I want you to *stop* thinking in those terms: ready, aim, and fire. There is no ready. There is no aim. There is no fire. It's all part of action, and they all happen at once. Because most people have several actions—personal and professional—happening at once. Nothing will ever be perfect, and you can't expect it to be. There was always a chance I would bomb that day, fail to connect with the audience, forget my words, or have my jokes fall flat. There is *always* a risk of failure. If there isn't, you're not aiming high enough. I simply refused to make the risks *bigger* than they were.

Was it the right opportunity for my vision for my execution platform? Worth my time? Right audience? Yes, yes, and yes. Why else would I leave my family and take time I didn't really have out of my weekend? When offered an incredible opportunity to further my goals, I acted—just as I had when I cut short our 10-year anniversary trip to stop in Singapore to begin the sale of my business. This was too big a moment to pass on. I wanted nothing more than to seize this opportunity to help people.

If my fellow speakers knew more about me and the way I execute, they might not have blanched at my seeming lack of preparation and readiness. Because I wasn't just ready. I was *prepared* for my debut on stage. I have learned to surround myself with people who can help make my actions successful. The few run-throughs I had done were in front of people I trusted to give me unfiltered feedback to make my points stronger and the content more organized. My slides were professional, and I had interactive handouts for the whole audience. In other words, my passion for the topic didn't make me irrational, and leading with action didn't make me reckless.

People who lead with action always know there is no time to get stuck in analysis paralysis. In this context, action isn't always about a grand strategy or a clear, step-by-step plan. I'm not discounting the importance of strategy and planning. I just know how easy it is to get stuck spending your time and energy planning rather than doing. No time for doubt or fear—for playing it safe and staying in my comfort zone.

So many ideas and businesses fail to act and execute because they wait for the "perfect time" to act and they try to time the market. Which no one can really do. There's never a perfect time. Bad timing can kill a great idea, but no one can completely control that—or even prevent it. The dot-com company I worked for in 1999 was like Dropbox. The vision was right, but the timing was wrong. That happens sometimes. Your steps might not lead where you hoped, and it's probably going to take more effort, time, and money than you expected. But you can't let that stop you from taking action. *You have little chance of success and finding the path that leads to a path if you don't move.*

You have even less if you doubt your potential and the potential of others to act. There is so much untapped and unknown potential out there—people who underestimate their capabilities. And this goes for the solo entrepreneur to the top of any organization. Doubt, like problems, is often just about scale. The problems you have as a startup and a $10 million company will often be the same problems you have as a $100 million company, just bigger.

. . . .

No one knows everything about what they
are doing when they act, and those who say
they do are either delusional or arrogant.

. . . .

Why do we think we should always be right? That we must
have all the answers? Because too many of us have been taught
that makes us strong. No. I'm always ready to admit I do not have
all the answers, and I consider other perspectives. That's not doubt.
That's power.

Opening myself up to other people's perspectives lowers my
resistance to change and helps me deal with the uncertainty that
could prevent me from doing many things. It sets me up for resilience. I won't let doubt stop me because I know it is an exagger-
ated, and on many occasions irrational, reaction. Just as I treat
fear, I don't let doubt get the better of me and prevent me from
taking the actions I need to take.

Yet that's about me: sheer willpower and emotional mastery
get me through most of my fear, doubt, and uncertainty. Here are
six other techniques for taking action that have helped me act
when I was faced with those emotions:

Six Techniques for Taking Action

1. Follow the 40-70 Rule.
2. Consider the worst-case scenario.
3. Find out what is missing.
4. Assess the risk of inaction.
5. Avoid the "when . . . then" trap.
6. Identify the best thing that could happen.

1. Follow the 40-70 Rule

One of the most common ways people get stuck in fear and doubt is focusing on their need for certainty. How to remedy this? I like General Colin Powell's "40-70 Rule." The essence of the rule is this: collect 40 to 70 percent of available facts and data, then go with your gut. Don't wait until you have enough facts to be 100 percent sure, or you'll be too late.

I've seen many companies fail because, unfortunately, they wanted that 100 percent certainty. That's not only fear of uncertainty talking but also wanting certainty in a world that is anything but certain. That's when the marketplace leaves you and your business behind. This is why you must execute faster than ever. Companies on the S&P 500 Index 50 years ago stayed on the index an average of 33 years. By 2026, that number is expected to be just 14 years.[1] There is always new competition or a killer app or innovation or a change in the market. There are new customers whom you have never served, new global partners that you can't understand, new generations you need to communicate with, and new ways of doing business that you don't learn in business school.

For example, early in my career, I invested in three similar companies at once because I believed their ideas were right for the market. I just did not know which one would execute better. Most people would not take that investment thesis, but I was only 40 percent certain, so I covered all my bets. In the end, one company went under and one was sold, which was a wash, but one is still going strong today. A decade later, faced with the same opportunity and knowing what I know now, I'd like to think I could get to 70 percent certainty in the same amount of time and just invest in two of the companies. But I wouldn't wait for absolute certainty to invest in just one because the valuation would have certainly gone up by the time I was able to make the decision.

2. Consider the Worst-Case Scenario

When I was about to buy my first house, I was worried that I couldn't afford it. My dad asked me, "What's the worst thing that could happen?" I thought about it. The worst thing that could happen was that I would have to give it back to the bank. "Can you handle that?" my dad asked. I could. I was willing to bet on myself and act even when thinking about the *worst* thing that could happen by taking that action.

If you can handle the worst-case scenario, then you know you can probably handle anything else in between. Remember: Your confidence in *you* (and your team) needs to be greater than anyone else's doubt—especially your own. It's a bet that you'll deliver on the promise of what you are doing.

3. Find out What Is Missing

Fear or doubt might be in the way, but there is often something missing that is not letting us feel "safe" taking action. Do you need to assess the pros and cons of the action? Write them down.

Do you need a clearer picture of how you are going to take your first step? Get that clarity from someone who has done it before. Are you someone who needs to know the next step before taking the first? Do you have a Plan B? Map them out. I know what I have needed was unconditional encouragement from my husband and family that if I failed, they'd be there to pick me up. What do you *need* to take action?

4. Assess the Risk of Inaction

Sometimes the risk of *not* taking action is actually greater than the risk of moving forward. Take a look at the risks or issues if you *don't* take the first and next steps. What would happen? What would the outcome look like 3, 6, or 12 months from now? Are they greater than the risk associated with taking it? Are you making those risks much worse than they actually are?

It's usually better to rock the boat than to die sinking in it— or watch someone else seize the day. If you don't see the competition in front of you, that means everyone is chasing you.

5. Avoid the When ... Then Trap

> When I have enough money, then I can start my own business.
> When I have more experience, then I'll go out on my own.
> When I get this next training, then I'll get started.
> When I get my website up, then I'll go get clients.
> When I have all the data, then I'll make a decision.

You know what these "when ... then" statements usually mean for action? Inaction. Someone once told me, "One day or someday is not a real day, like Monday or Tuesday." It's all a trap for inaction—for playing it safe and getting distracted by thinking too long about things too far ahead.

It's too easy to wait for all the data to take that first step. Action is just like exercise: The first step is to move. Get out of your head, and act to execute your vision. Thinking about the things that might happen is essential for adaptation and anticipation, but too much leads to analysis paralysis. There are always exceptions to the rule, but you can't play for the exceptions (or contingencies or possibilities). You can just prepare for them. If you keep playing for the exceptions—just as if you always planned for the future without taking care to grow in the present—you will never play for the realities. When you think about all the possibilities, you actually end up putting off action.

6. Identify the Best Thing That Could Happen

There are lots of things that could happen, and we can't always stop thinking about them. I need to remind my team of this sometimes: There is always going to be risk. There's always going to be something that might happen. Why not think about the *great* things that could happen if you take action? What are the possibilities? What doors would open? At times, that risk might be too great, but when there's no risk, there's usually little opportunity for growth. You execute, but you get a lower return or results. That's thinking and acting too small.

We should be thinking about what the opportunities are and act. That's how I grew my business to where it is today: by never being afraid to take that first step.

The best things happen when you do.

ACTION CHECK

Questions for Self-Reflection

Consider a time in the past when you had fear or doubt but you took action anyway.

How did you feel?

What was the outcome?

How can you use that feeling now?

Consider a time in the past when you had fear or doubt but you failed to act.

What stopped you and why?

Is this what usually gets in the way of your taking action? Is that what's stopping you right now from taking action?

How could you move past this uncertainty?

Action—Trait Summary and Real-Life Scenario

ACTION: REFLECTIONS AND MOVING FORWARD

- Action is the linchpin for the five traits of execution. It's the trait around which all the others revolve.
- Action reminds you to check your vision and fulfill your passion.
- Action creates more opportunities—not just for growth but to be strong and resilient and to form relationships so that you can scale your execution.
- There's no substitute for taking action.
- Sure, you can always find reasons to wait, delay, and avoid, but you're wasting time and energy. Remember that until you act, all your analyses and projections are approximations and guesswork. You don't know what will happen until you start.
- As human beings, we tend to err on the side of caution, and we overvalue fear and doubt. It is essential that you do not let these biases—and they are biases—stop you from taking the first and next steps.
- Learn how to put the doubts and fears and uncertainty to one side, address them head-on, or keep them in perspective and act anyway.
- Always make sure that your action steps are aligned with your vision and capture your passion and emotional commitment—to yourself and those you care about. When

they are aligned, they will be more meaningful, compelling you to take action and ensuring that you appreciate the value of every step.

- All that will be extremely important, especially managing emotions, as you develop the traits of resilience and create relationships and gain a balanced perspective on action and execution.

BEFORE YOU GO: WHAT'S THE SCENARIO?

This scenario is designed to help you think about everything you have learned in this section. Please take a few minutes to complete this exercise as best you can. I promise it will be worth it. If you get stuck or are not sure about your answer, go back and review the section. Remember, there is no right or wrong answer here. This is just a way of applying your new knowledge on action.

Often it is easier to give advice to someone else, when you're not wrapped up in your own world, full of all its complexities. A highly successful executive wants to leave her job and start her own business. She's excited because she feels this new venture will be great for her and her family, and it will give her the opportunity to make a real difference. But she's scared and doesn't know where to start.

What step would you advise her to take first? How would you advise her to act?

TRAIT 4

RESILIENCE

Dealing with Obstacles, Change, and Uncertainty

*Genius is 1 percent inspiration and
99 percent perspiration.*

—THOMAS EDISON

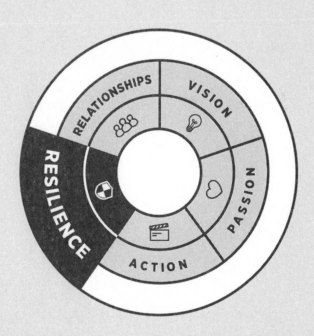

14

Life Rarely Goes as Planned

The day our twins came was the best and worst day of my life. I had always dreamed of having a large family. My father's parents were married over 60 years, had five boys, 16 grandkids, and 28 great-grandkids. My childhood was filled with family reunions at which each family would wear color-coded polo shirts, ours in a bright blue. We looked like a box of crayons—one my husband and I wanted to add our color to.

We had been together for over a decade when I sold my first company in 2008. It was then that having a family became the new North Star for the life I wanted. We were young, healthy, and happy. Our families had no history of infertility. We followed all the advice for emotionally and physically preparing to get pregnant. Neither of us thought for a moment we would run into any problems.

Until we did.

When I initially failed to get pregnant, we knew starting our family wouldn't be as simple as we had hoped. But we kept trying.

Time crept by at a painful pace. Weeks became months and months became years. After countless visits to doctors, we had no explanation. We were devastated, but quickly came to terms with the fact that our journey to parenthood—like any successful journey—was going to be more difficult than most. We would not be deterred by some inconclusive tests in our quest for a bigger family.

We decided to try in vitro fertilization (IVF), which included blood tests, ultrasounds, daily shots, and surgery. Most women have few complications from these procedures, so I assumed I wouldn't be much different. I had my egg retrieval surgery on a Monday morning, and with my doctor's permission I boarded a plane to Aspen Tuesday afternoon to attend my company's annual executive off-site meeting.

I was feeling a little fatigued when I left my house, but I was sure it was just a result of the hormone drugs. I was wrong. Over the next 48 hours, liters of fluid filled and distended my abdomen. I couldn't eat anything, and I soon became violently ill. I had never been so sick or terrified in my life. I called my husband and told him I would get on the next plane back to San Diego, which connected through Los Angeles. But by the time I got to LAX, the pain was so disorienting I couldn't think straight, let alone wait hours for another flight. I was really hurting, and I just needed to get home, so I took a taxi back to San Diego, passed out in the backseat.

When I arrived home, I could barely speak or move. My husband immediately rushed me to the emergency room. The hospital quickly determined I was suffering from ovarian hyperstimulation syndrome. It's caused by fertility drugs, and most cases are mild. Mine was severe, and if it had been left untreated for much longer, it could have killed me. I was immediately checked into an operating room where a tap drained the fluid from my abdomen. After a couple of days of bed rest and fluids, I regained my energy and optimism. The doctors said there was no reason I could not continue to try IVF with closer monitoring. I was more committed than ever to ensure I did everything I could to turn my vision of having a family with my husband into a beautiful reality.

We spent the next two years doing the IVF procedures, all with no success. After sharing our story with a close friend, he mentioned that he knew someone who had a surrogate carry their twins. *Wait, surrogate?* Of course I had heard of surrogacy, but I didn't know anything about the clinical details. When I had dreamed about my journey of becoming a mother, I had always assumed I would be the one to carry my own child. But we had already gone through so much pain and disappointment. Surrogacy offered us a different direction—a new opportunity. We spent the next year with lawyers, physiatrists, and potential surrogates until we finally found the perfect match: Jennifer. She lived in San Diego, and we could attend all of her doctors' appointments and be there for the delivery.

Surrogacy was not the pregnancy I had imagined on our journey to parenthood, but the end result would be the same: a family of our own. When we got the amazing news we were having twins, we were over the moon! But given the roller coaster we had been on, my husband and I agreed to wait until well into the second trimester to share the news outside our immediate family. And that was fine because I had plenty going on to occupy my mind.

During Jennifer's (and my) pregnancy, my deal with the Singaporean company I was trying to sell to heated up. We went into full-blown due diligence—a very time-consuming process that can go for months on end. Meetings with lawyers and bankers consumed almost the entirety of my days and nights. But I had the note with my vision to sell my company on my bathroom mirror to keep me going. And now there was a perfect and much anticipated addition: the ultrasound picture of our two little ones. I had it with me at all times to remind myself that the sleepless nights were *worth it*.

If all went as I had imagined, I would have plenty of time to enjoy and commit to both momentous events. The target closing date for the deal was April. The twins weren't expected until August.

Nothing went as planned.

A sudden infection forced our surrogate into the hospital at 20 weeks, bedridden. The infection got worse over the next month, and the doctors were forced to deliver our twins at 24 weeks—three and a half months before their due date. I never got to hold my babies or even touch them after they were born. Both weighed only a pound and were immediately whisked away to neonatal intensive care unit. My son had a staph infection and brain bleed, and my daughter needed open-heart surgery.

I had been relentlessly tough in the face of so many setbacks and obstacles in my life, but nothing had prepared me for this nightmare. Neither my husband nor I had ever seen anything worse or heard anything more awful than our doctors telling us in the kindest way possible that there was a good chance one or both of our babies wouldn't survive. Even if they did make it, they were so underdeveloped they could be disabled for life. It's hard to describe in words. We felt . . . immobile.

The first time we touched our children was through the hand holes of an incubator in the NICU. Their tiny hands were barely big or strong enough to wrap around our fingers. No one should ever have to see tubes and wires running from their babies' fragile bodies to screens and machines. No one should ever see their children attached to machines keeping them alive, feeding them, monitoring their vital signs, giving them oxygen . . . you don't want to think about losing them. Even when every doctor has told you the worst-case scenario is "more than possible," you can't give up hope.

There wasn't a single day in the 14 weeks that I didn't fear one or both of my twins was going to die. There were days I didn't want to get out of bed, let alone go to work, but I had no choice. I had two little babies who needed me as they fought for their lives, and hundreds of employees and their families counting on me to close the biggest deal of my life with a company halfway around the world.

While my husband and I never dismissed the possibility of the worst-case scenario, we refused to focus on it. Even with all the stress and uncertainty, we kept an overall positive outlook. We never gave up. We persevered—for each other and them. We had no choice but to be strong so they could feel our strength, prayers, and love to overcome the odds.

We hid our pain from the world. Outside of our immediate family, no one still had any idea of the pain we were going through. No one saw my broken heart at work. No one heard about the countless nights I cried myself to sleep. Or the drastic ups and downs I experienced during the daily health updates. The same was true about my deal. As my children fought for their lives, the deal had dragged, and we had missed our April closing date. We were now well into May, jeopardizing the vision I had on the note taped to my bathroom mirror. But I wouldn't let my team feel the constant and crushing pressure I was under to close the deal and get back to the hospital to be with my children. *I had to be strong.*

Over the following months, my visions became reality: the deal closed, and our twins' health stabilized. They were fighters. When we were finally able to bring them home from the hospital, we threw a surprise party to introduce them to our friends. I'm sure you can imagine their reaction: *"What? You have twins? How could you have not told anyone?"*

The truth was, our experience was too painful to share with more than the few people we needed to get us through. I have never felt so vulnerable. Those days challenged my faith and optimism to a near paralyzing degree. So much so that it hurts to talk (and write) about it today. But I now realize our twins showed us true resilience and brought it out in us. They helped us surmount the insurmountable. Reminded us to find strength when we were powerless and helpless. To persevere when the odds said that failing was more than an option. To believe in the possibilities when uncertainty was all we had.

············

Often the only thing certain
in life is uncertainty.

············

The truth is that few of us will face moments like ours with the birth of our twins. We haven't since. Most tests of my resilience have looked more like the time when the first company

I worked for went bankrupt. Not literal life-and-death circumstances, just life not going as planned when you try to execute. The easy choice is always to give up. The path I chose when our twins were born was to continue believing in the possibilities and to have the emotional endurance to move forward despite the pain and hardship.

This is what it means to master resilience. This is what you need as you encounter your own obstacles, setbacks, and failures in executing your vision.

RESILIENCE CHECK

Questions for Self-Reflection

What are the biggest obstacles standing in the way of your success and executing your vision? Take some time to think about that before we dive into the details of resilience and execution. Then think about you and your strengths when it comes to resilience.

How do you typically feel when things don't go according to plan and you don't get the results you had hoped for? For example, were you feeling frustrated, guilty, energized, or stressed?

What do you typically do when things don't go according to plan and you don't get the results you had hoped for?

15

Bouncing Back After Setbacks

I was at IKEA on a weekend in 2006 when I got the phone call from my tech guy: our server had failed and could not be fixed. We were operating on a bare-bones budget, and a backup server was too expensive. Now our database was gone, the data unrecoverable.

My heart dropped. I thought it was the end of my company. That one server represented the entirety of the business. There *was* no business without it. A small part of me thought about folding—closing up shop, making excuses, forgetting this ever happened, and getting out. I was in full panic mode as I searched to find an exit from the never-ending IKEA maze of living and dining rooms and floor samples of what things look like when all the screws are in the right place, desperately trying to think of what to do next for my collapsing company. This was a major error and oversight, and I took full responsibility as CEO.

First thing Monday, I risked embarrassment, yelling, and worse. I personally reached out to our clients one by one to explain what had happened. I blamed no one but me, and asked for their patience and support while we got back up and running. I promised to never make the same mistake again. I hoped that our good work and relationships with them would give them confidence that we would rebuild better than before and that we were determined to do so. We had already bought a new server *and* a backup, and we would work around the clock until we were up and running.

Not a single advertising client deserted us that day or in the weeks that it took to get our marketing platform running again. I was transparent about the situation from the beginning, and I honored my promise of doing everything we could to fix it. I contacted our clients and bared my soul. I explained our solution—to rebuild and install a backup source—and asked if they would send me a copy of the data I had lost. Even with a few new gray hairs and more sleepless nights, I felt uplifted. I had not succumbed to the temptation to hide any of the truth when faced with this setback or play the blame game as I put the crisis behind us.

And I was better for it.

Something like my server crash happens to everyone who is trying to achieve anything, and it will *inevitably* happen to you as you execute on your vision. In executing in business and in life, it's rare that everything runs completely according to plan. Yet research has shown that people are overly optimistic in their predictions about their ability to complete a task. It's very common to ignore or discount the fact that obstacles will arise, leading to execution problems when the unexpected occurs, so:

- Remember what my grandfather told me. Everything takes twice as long, costs twice as much, and takes twice as much energy as you anticipate. You should expect complications, delays, drama, rejection, and chaos on the path to success— and prepare for all of that.

- Remember the drawings of what success really looks like. You must find a way forward through the ups and downs even if it means throwing your plan away and making a new one when the situation calls for it.

And if you fail? So what! At least you go down swinging. When faced with defeat, the easiest thing to do is to quit or play it safe the next time you execute. *No!* There's a reason why the classic hero's journey involves overcoming obstacles to achieve a goal. There is something noble and universal in meeting all challenges and rising above setbacks, obstacles, and failures. That kind of success helps define you as a hero—to yourself as well as others.

Not as a savior but a hero of execution.

RESILIENCE CHECK

Questions for Self-Reflection

How do you typically **feel** when things don't go according to plan and you don't get the results you had hoped for (for example, frustrated, guilty, energized, or stressed)?

What do you typically **do** when things don't go according to plan and you don't get the results you had hoped for? Explain the strategies behind those actions.

Think about the last time you faced failure, serious challenges, or a major setback. How did you **react**? What did you **learn**?

16

Fail Forward

According to an article published on Bloomberg.com, people who have previously failed have doubled their chances of success the next time around compared to first-time entrepreneurs.[1] Failure—and accepting it—is part of success. I'm living proof.

Like many entrepreneurs, I encountered failures like my server breakdown early in my career. You and your team will attempt things that will fail, and you will need to adapt to change. Understanding the inevitability and power of those failures has been vital to executing in my own career and fundamental to building a company in a growing and dynamic market. In fact, I believe if failure doesn't happen to you—if you're not failing and bouncing back constantly—you're not trying hard enough! I still fail all the time. Really! Failure just has a different scale and feel to me today.

Resilient people "fail forward" and thrive in the process of change. Knock them down 9 times and they'll get up 10 times. Not only will they get up but they'll get up stronger and wiser:

- Being resilient means anticipating change and adapting accordingly. Resilience isn't just about dealing with obstacles, crises, and setbacks. It's about dealing with them *in constructive, creative ways.*

- Being resilient means understanding that difficulties not only are going to occur but also offer the best opportunities for growth. No one loves to hit dead ends, but the resilient among us know how to uncover possibilities while holding on to their purpose, staying true to themselves, and believing in themselves and their teams. This makes them inspiring and calming individuals when situations are intense or chaotic.
- Being resilient means accepting that setbacks can be overwhelming and can lead to uncomfortable emotions. Was I embarrassed when I had to call all my clients when our server crashed? I was mortified. But I moved forward anyway and showed my team the way.

All of that is why resilience is a key factor for personal and professional success when that line to the top gets really messy. In a study sponsored by Nationwide and Vodafone, nearly 100 percent of participants cited resilience as a factor in their success.[2] It works the other way too. An Accenture survey reported that 71 percent of executives valued resilience in employees when deciding whom to hire and retain.[3]

Without resilience, we are at the mercy of the universe. We're left feeling battered by the unexpected, overcome with emotions, and incapable of making decisions. Yet adding an ounce or two of fortitude and self-determination to our lifestyle flips the script. Suddenly, we can fail and come back stronger. We can accept life's uncomfortable, even tragic lessons and use them as stepping stones. We see this every day in the way our people and our world respond to national tragedies and natural disasters when we pull together to help others and be our resilient best and find a way forward.

Doing that requires focusing on these key areas that are essential to resilience and execution:

- **Developing a growth mindset:** This is the cognitive ability to perceive things differently.
- **Developing a growth heartset:** This is the emotional endurance to keep going so that creativity, adaptation, and innovation can thrive even in the face of failure and you still have the courage and will to keep going.
- **Practicing how to be resilient:** Because like any muscle in your body, you build and develop it through exercise.

Just remember as we move forward in this section, if you lead with resilience, your biggest weakness can be the overuse of your strength.

You Might Never Give Up, Even When You Should

Not all circumstances have good outcomes or possibilities. There are true dead ends, mistakes that you cannot fully recover from, and times you must move in a different direction than you initially expected. Make sure you know when to let go.

You Might Stop Seeing Opportunities, Even When You Shouldn't

Resilient people course correct easily, but they can get caught up in their passion and action when executing a solution. Don't get *too* focused on what you're doing and thus miss a different direction and bigger opportunities. Make sure you know when to move on.

You Might See Too Many Possibilities When You Really Need to Focus

Resilient people thrive in chaos and have a natural instinct to pivot. *But* don't pivot so fast that you fail to see an idea all the way through. Fight the boredom to always change. Be resilient, be adaptive, and be creative, but don't course correct to oblivion. Make sure you know when to stay the course.

. . .

OK, ready? Let's get going and build your resilience so you can keep moving forward. Learning to overcome challenges, obstacles, setbacks, and failures that come your way will lead to your greatest opportunities for adaptation, learning, and growth.

RESILIENCE CHECK

Questions for Self-Reflection

For one day, challenge your thinking. Be the devil's advocate. Think differently. Take the opposite view and make a case for alternative positions. Then take a step back.

What did you learn from this exercise?

What will you now do differently as a result?

17

Minds and Hearts

B eing 23 and having to lay off my colleagues, some of whom were my dearest friends, only to be let go myself was one of the most challenging times in my life. It didn't matter that I knew I had done the best I could and controlled everything that was possible to control. Ultimately, none of us had jobs, and I'd let people down. I felt like a failure. The emotional weight was heavy.

As I saw it, I had two options. I could get swept up in my sadness, be depressed, and ruminate about what we could have done differently. Or I could find a way to move forward. I had tried to do that before the bubble burst by finding new revenue streams. When that failed, I resolved to build something that wouldn't have that same outcome, and started my first company.

In doing so, I took control of the two sides of resilience to execute: mindset and heartset.

Mindset: Challenging the Status Quo

In *Mindset*, Carol Dweck's classic book on the psychology of success, she talks about the difference between a "fixed" and a "growth" mindset. Someone with a fixed mindset believes in limitations and believes that change is painful and difficult. Someone with a growth mindset recognizes that change is not only possible but also a driver of creativity and success. In today's ever-changing world, adaptation is vital. So resilience is also about having a mindset that allows for creativity and adaptation: a growth mindset.

A growth mindset means that in every situation, there is an opportunity to learn and see things differently. It involves always challenging the status quo and considering many possible avenues. It is the constant search beyond the obvious and an open-mindedness to consider alternatives to every problem and situation.

What if you challenged the status quo and saw everything before you as an opportunity? Even stumbling blocks would appear to be steps up. That's the mindset of entrepreneurs who know that the five-year industry failure rate hovers at around 50 percent, as evidenced by a Statistic Brain study.[1] Does that stop this resilient crowd? Not a chance!

To become resilient, you must be open to the same possibilities, fostering growth. As you meet challenges, even those that seem insurmountable, you must begin to consider them from new and multiple perspectives. Give yourself a bird's-eye view. Yesterday's failure can become tomorrow's success if you take the right path. Arianna Huffington had the doors to publishing slammed in her face over and over when her second book was rejected more than 30 times. Then she had the doors to elected office slammed in her face when she lost her California gubernatorial bid. But as the saying goes, those closed doors opened a window for a new venture in 2005: *HuffPost*, today one of the most powerful platforms in the world.

By being open-minded and developing a growth mindset that is not fixed on the obvious, you can train yourself to see different perspectives on any issue, which will allow you to formulate new solutions to almost any problem. This will serve you well when things don't go according to plan. Conversely, having a growth mindset will also serve you well when things *are* going well and there is seemingly no reason to adapt or be resilient because no changes are needed. In fact, when the only thing certain is uncertainty, that's when adaptability is crucial: when you don't know what you don't know. That's when you need your growth mindset to make you stronger.

Look at Jeff Bezos. Remember when Amazon was just a disruptive bookseller? Yet Bezos has done more than disrupt various businesses to become the third largest retailer in the world. He has fundamentally disrupted the way business is done. He cared less about what Wall Street thought and more about investing to grow the business into new areas like cloud computing.

Resilience Pulse Check

Take a situation you are experiencing right now that is a *problem or crisis*. How could the concept of having a growth mindset help you think differently and execute better?

Now, think of something that is going really well— where you are **succeeding**. How could you use this concept of a growth mindset to help you identify how it could be even better?

But just because you succeed with a growth mindset doesn't mean you can then leave your heart behind. A growth mindset that allows you to learn from failure but have the courage to keep moving in the face of failure requires a growth *heartset*. You need a growth mindset if you're going to be disruptive. You need a growth heartset to stay human.

Heartset: Emotional Strength in the Face of Difficulties

Despite the risks I faced when I started my first company, I had the mindset to seize the opportunity to act. But I needed my heartset to be emotionally resilient as I set out to create something of my own. And that heartset was tested. Many times when I was working to grow the company, I had to use my personal savings and max out my credit cards to cover payroll. I even worked without pay for an entire year because I knew deep in my heart we would be successful.

Almost all entrepreneurs and leaders have a similar story of how their heartset pulled them through the tough times. When the music site Pandora faced corporate bankruptcy in 2001, its founder Tim Westergren wouldn't give up and still believed he could make it. His heartset was so strong that 50 employees felt it and agreed to work without pay until the company could escape its fiscal hole. It took two years and dozens of heartfelt speeches to pump up his people and keep them pushing forward to reach that goal.

The team's resilience in the face of failure paid off in the end. Like Westergren himself, his people probably had to max out their credit cards and put off paying bills. Who knows how many of them crashed on a friend's sofa for too long or lived with their parents? But that's what heartset does. It pushes you further than you thought you could go when you believe and *feel* you are executing on something great—even when prudence says quit and the emotional and fiscal stress is strong.

Westergren himself doesn't advise entrepreneurs to do this (and what he did is actually illegal in California, which he didn't realize at the time). Still I understand wanting to push past that emotional stress. Since those early days of my company and despite being secure in my vision, I still go through emotional stress all the time. It's a daily event. It would destroy me if I let it. I need my heartset to stay positive, even in the face of problems and crises that affect the growth of the company.

Heartset is the ability to find emotional strength in the face of difficulties—the feelings that keep our growth mindset from being too cold, too mean, and too lacking in kindness or even humanity.

Consider this lesson from Elon Musk. Before he was a billionaire inventor and entrepreneur, Elon Musk failed many times. In 1996, he was kicked out of the company he had founded with his brother. After that, his first iteration of PayPal was identified as a terrible business idea. His Tesla vehicles have come under scrutiny, while several of his SpaceX rocket launches have exploded. But through all this, Musk has been determined to succeed. After each of his failures, he has dusted himself off and looked to the future for growth, and has found success, including successful rocket launches in 2018.

That's what the people and organizations who invest in his success expect him to do: execute in spite of any failures or setbacks. In fact, despite those explosions and before the recent rockets that made it into space, SpaceX signed an agreement with NASA—the first deal of its kind made with a private citizen.

Musk is now worth more than $20 billion, and his products are known all over the world. But I never knew the depth of his heartset until he showed his heart to the people who work for him. In 2017, an e-mail he wrote to the team at Tesla was posted online. Musk wrote it after he learned about the high rate of injuries being reported at his Freemont, California, plant. He said he would personally get involved on the line to encourage transparency in reporting. He even told the team that he would perform the same tasks as the people who were getting injured:

> Going forward, I've asked that every injury be reported directly to me, without exception. I'm meeting with the safety team every week and would like to meet every injured person as soon as they are well, so that I can understand from them exactly what we need to do to make it better. I will then go down to the production line and perform the same task that they perform. This is what all managers at Tesla should do as a matter of course. At Tesla, we lead from the front line, not from some safe and comfortable ivory tower.[2]

Sure, paying attention to workers has a long connection to worker productivity, but fidelity to those workers does not. So many leaders talk about creating connected and collaborative work environments, but those environments turn out to be toxic for the workers and fall apart when the bottom line stops growing, problems surface, or accusations of corruption, discrimination, and harassment arise. These leaders and their organizations lack heartset and thus resilience. An e-mail from those leaders in Musk's position might be scoffed at as "too little too late" and a publicity ploy. Musk's words weren't met with skepticism because he already had created a culture of resiliency that had heartset.

Musk's e-mail is a lesson on how essential it is to stay connected top to bottom so that when your resiliency is tested, your people already know that you care about what it is before you step foot on that line. His heartset made his people feel his passion for what Tesla was doing and fight through the problems.

He channeled his heartset into a problem and turned an absolute negative into a chance for something positive.

Here's what I've learned to do for myself when fear, anxiety, frustration, and stress creep in. I find something else I feel connected to and passionate about. I don't wallow in it. When I'm out of control in one situation, I look for stability in another area of my life. I focus on things that are positive, inspiring, and uplifting for me.

When I feel overwhelmed, I make it a priority to focus on things that relieve stress like playing with my twins, taking a spin class, or having lunch with a friend. As a CEO, I often deal with significant stress and uncertainty, so I have learned to compartmentalize when things get crazy such as during the acquisition of another company. There are some decisions I can't control because I am working with so many parties. In fact, I don't always have control of the outcome—acquisitions sometimes fall apart for many reasons (for example, money, state of the market, or lack of agreement from the board and shareholders). That's when

I step back and remember not to take things personally. I have learned that in certain situations, it may be best to remove myself from the situation completely.

The hardest part for me is to forgive myself even when others cannot. I can't get weighed down in what didn't work. It's quicksand. When others are upset and angry with a decision I've made or a direction I'm taking, I must be able to step back and ask myself, "Is what I'm doing right and for the greater good?" My dad always said, "At the end of the day, you have to know that you did the best you could. That's all you can do." I must know in my mind *and my heart*.

That said, if you're generally fulfilled, you can avoid wallowing too long in difficult situations. Plus, you will be able to say, "I did my best, and that was all I could do"—and you'll mean it.

Simply put, your mind isn't the only part of your body that must become resilient; your heart should too. Your emotional responses are keys to resilience. Human beings tend to overestimate fear because we are programmed for survival and our brain and nervous system are sensitive to threats. Obstacles, setbacks, and failures can hurt. They cause fear and a host of negatively perceived reactions like shame, guilt, anger, frustration, and self-doubt. Managing these emotions will enable you to take action. It also allows you to adapt and take action to move forward with heart.

This kind of emotion management is not just the key to resilience and execution. It's the key to success in many areas of life. What do you do to proactively understand and manage your emotions? There are various ways to attend to your emotions constructively, including those I just mentioned. Which of these resonate for you?

- Exercise
- Talking to a mentor or friend
- Meditating
- Creating a plan
- Taking a step toward fixing it
- Identifying what you can control
- Compartmentalizing
- Removing yourself from the situation (when possible)

Resilience Pulse Check

On a scale from 1 to 10, how good are you at managing your heartset? What productive actions do you take to manage your emotions (for example, exercising, talking with someone, journaling, meditating, or devising a plan)? In hindsight, what else could you have done to manage your emotions more constructively?

Or if you want a more visual lesson, stream the original *Rocky*. After several sequels in which Sylvester Stallone's Rocky Balboa vanquishes every opponent in the end, it is sometimes hard to remember that in the original movie, Rocky *loses*. The film didn't. It won Best Picture and Best Screenplay for Stallone at the Oscars—but Rocky did.

But do you think of him as a loser? I don't. To me, Rocky is the ultimate demonstration of heartset. He has the emotional endurance to make it to the end. Yes, he needed to demonstrate mindset. He had to learn to adapt to Apollo, find his weakness, and attack it. What I remember, however, is not that mindset but his heartset—his courage and ability to stay positive even when his vision literally and figuratively was blurred and bloodied. When knocked down 9 times, Rocky got up 10.

People who have this heartset will always feel successful in their execution. They may not always win, but they never get knocked out. Especially when they practice it day in and day out.

Questions for Self-Reflection

Think of a time when you faced a setback, obstacle, or failure.

What was your initial reaction, and how did you manage your reaction to it?

Did you use a growth mindset *and* heartset? If so, how? If not, and faced with the same situation again, what would you do differently?

18

Practicing and Preparing for Resilience

Just months after buying my red Jeep when I was 16, I crashed it. It was totally my fault. I couldn't afford to put a stereo in the Jeep, and since my vision involved listening to tunes with my friends, I had put my boom box in the car. Alone in the car one day, I reached down to change my cassette tape, took my eyes off the road for just a few seconds, and as I looked up, I hit another car. No one was injured. The other car wasn't badly banged up. Mine, not so much.

I sat by the side of the road on top of my Jeep just crying as the police and tow truck came. My Jeep wasn't totaled, but the front looked like an accordion. I couldn't afford the deductible to repair it, so my dad, who knew a lot about self-service auto repair from his first business, tried to stretch it out with a bulldozer. He tied the back of the car to a tree and pulled on the front with the bulldozer to un-squish it. He then hammered out the fender and made it look straight. It looked like . . . a Jeep that had been in a car wreck and then fixed by a bulldozer, a hammer, and my dad in our backyard.

When you're 16-year-old girl, you care about how things look. I tried to cover the ugliness up. I bought a "bra" for the front to make it look snazzy. But what was I going to do? I had crashed my car. It was my fault. This was long before anyone talked about the dangers of distracted driving—a lesson I had now learned on my own. I had two choices: wallow in pity and start taking the bus to school, or suck it up, accept responsibility, start driving again, and resolve never to drive distracted again.

I chose the latter.

More than 20 years later as I was writing this book, I found myself stranded by the side of another road—this time the break-down lane on the I-880 outside San Francisco. Only it wasn't my fault. My Uber had broken down on the way to the airport, and we were already running late. As I felt the stress of the day rise and my full schedule waiting for me upon my return to San Diego, I started to feel overwhelmed. I had no idea what to do.

That's when I remembered the story of my Jeep and how I felt sitting on the hood, crying. And I realized I had two choices: let the stress of a situation that I had no control over overwhelm me or get out of the car and hitchhike.

I chose the latter.

I got out of the car in the breakdown lane and stood by the side of the car thumbing for a ride in my work clothes. I have the picture my Uber driver took to prove it! And with temperatures approaching 90 degrees, the road shimmering from the heat, I thought maybe someone might take pity on me.

"I am not going to bug you or rob you. I just need a lift to the airport!" I screamed as if the people in the cars whizzing by could hear me. No one stopped.

But if you look at my face in that picture? I'm smiling. I realized I needed to make the best of my situation, and if I missed my flight? Well, that's life, right? No need to take it out on myself, my Uber driver, or anyone else.

In both the Jeep and the Uber situations, I did what we all must do when life gets in the way: practice resilience.

**You must develop resilience
before you need it.**

You don't need resilience only when facing setbacks; it needs to become an innate part of who you are. In the same way that you don't want your first fire drill to be when there's a real fire, resilience needs to be developed before a crisis or a failure occurs. And just like pretty much everything else in life, practice makes perfect. Think of resilience—your mindset and heartset—as a muscle, and just like any muscle you want to build, you need to exercise it in order to execute at the highest level. It must become your reflex.

The good news is you can exercise it pretty much anywhere. Opportunities present themselves not just in a big loss, a minicrisis at work, or a tough setback but everywhere. Even when you think there is nothing you can do to make it better but smile.

Using Your Mindset and
Heartset Every Day

I love Guns N' Roses, and when they reunited in 2016, I decided to take 20 people from our leadership team to the show. I assumed the seats we ordered would be together. Nope. We picked them up at will-call, and *all 20* were single tickets scattered throughout the stadium. Welcome to the jungle . . . of disappointment.

We had a few choices in that moment. The first was to quit—just say *c'est la vie* and find something else fun to do.

The second was to enjoy it individually but start a group chat so we could share the experience collectively.

Then we realized there was a third choice, one that allowed us to practice a resilient mindset and get what we wanted on the first place. We made it a game to get all 20 of us together. We spent the next hour trying to change seats. We used our best negotiation skills until all 20 of us were sitting together. Our worst-made plan turned into a best-laid moment of collective fun—all because we took the opportunity to practice our resiliency. Paradise City!

Whether acting alone or as part of a team, resilience is nothing without perseverance and self-belief. If we didn't think we could do what we did at the concert—make a seemingly impossible challenge possible—then what would make us think we were going to fare better when we wanted to achieve our biggest dreams at home or our ambitious sales targets at work?

Adapting to challenges, dealing with stress, managing rejection, and handling or delivering bad news are things we all must face and do well to execute at the highest level. Those are exactly the times when you can practice resilience and gain the confidence you need to keep pushing forward through the toughest times and uncertainty. If *you* don't believe you can succeed, why should the people working with you?

. . . .

To adapt to challenges and setbacks,
you must be willing to do
whatever it takes to move forward.

. . . .

When I started my first business at my kitchen table, it was no romance, but it was certainly more romantic than where we ended up when I moved out of my kitchen and opened my first official office. I didn't have the money to set it up on my own, so we literally worked in our friend's company's storage closet. There were no windows, and it was meant to store printers and office supplies. It had about enough room to squeeze in four desks. There were two of us in there for a year.

When we started to grow, we interviewed people in the front lobby, and when they were hired, made them sit in the closet too until we moved. Was it uncomfortable? Of course! It was hot, there were no windows, and we couldn't move without bumping into something or each other. But comfort is not the point when practicing resilience. As I said in Trait 3, "Action," we all like the safety and comfort of easy choices, but that is not where the magic happens. From those days in the storage closet, I learned that if I'm not willing to be uncomfortable, I know I am not growing. That's why I make a habit of putting myself in the face of rejection all the time. That's how I grow, adjust, and build my resilience to face the day-to-day stresses. My only goal since the storage closet days has been to make sure my team felt less discomfort than I did but not be afraid of that discomfort.

When it comes to uncomfortable and stressful situations, the best lesson in resilience comes from people on the front lines, especially those who deal with customers. It's a big reason Southwest Airlines likes to recruit teachers for frontline positions—they know how to be resilient from the stress of working with kids in a classroom. It doesn't matter that teachers don't know anything about the airline business. The difference between teachers and other candidates is the teachers' ability to deal with the stress of the job while also dealing with cranky passengers acting like difficult students.

In other words, the best teachers have usually made resilience a habit through everyday practice.

In *The Power of Habit*, Charles Duhigg talks about how creating habits to deal with challenging situations is a cornerstone for success. For example, a big part of Starbucks' training for its employees is understanding and anticipating that customers will be upset at some point. Something will go wrong, or the wait will be endless for that latte, or someone will project his or her bad day onto you. So the company trains employees how to emotionally—and mentally—handle those situations by practicing them. Like pilots in flight simulators learning to handle extreme situations when lives are in the balance, Starbucks' baristas practice your disappointment with your Frappuccino. The more they practice, the more they develop resilience, and the more they have a mindset and heartset, which allows them to handle those situations better, faster, or before they even happen.[1]

The baristas also learn to be aware and accept responsibility if it is indeed their fault. In this way, Starbucks' "teams" on field behind the counter are no different from the best teams and players in sports. The best athletes spend hours practicing and training each day to improve their performance. Do you? Does your team?

Resilience Pulse Check

For one week, put yourself in a position each day where you have a high chance to get rejected and can practice being resilient. Ideas include these:

- Making a call you're worried about making
- Introducing yourself to someone new or striking up a conversation with a stranger
- Sharing an opinion you believe in that might not be the group consensus
- Doing anything out of your comfort zone

Keep a journal about each experience. At the end of each day, answer these questions: What have you learned? How could you perceive or handle things differently? What mistake or misstep did you take, and what did you learn from it? What will you do the next time you're in the situation?

What are you doing to set yourself and your people up to effectively adapt to challenges and setbacks in order to execute better when the problems happen? Remember: Developing resilience in one area of your life develops resilience in all areas of your life. Being resilient in your personal life transfers to your professional roles and vice versa. Your brain doesn't distinguish between these different areas of life.

Which means there is always a chance you will take something personally when handling rejection and failure. *Don't.*

From applying for a job to trying to make a reservation to not getting a response to a text or e-mail, we all face rejection sometimes. Deal with it. Stop projecting what you feel on the actions of others. If it wasn't an expressly personal attack, don't take it that way. Only by working to not take it personally when you are rejected or you fail or you just disagree with something or someone can you truly keep a balanced perspective about situations that challenge you.

And when it comes to the naysayers trying to bring you down? Don't let them. Naysayers, rejection, failure, uncomfortable situations . . . don't just deal with them. Seek them out! I make a habit of putting myself in the face of potential rejection all the time. It is how I know I am pushing myself as hard as I can and how I know that whatever happens, it will be OK. Does it help that I now have the money to back whatever decision I make? Of course! But I didn't always have the money I have today, and I have learned to never let money prevent me from practicing resilience—you have to save to prepare to *be* resilient.

My dad taught me that. After that startup failed and I was broke at 23, he told me to start saving so I would eventually have "F--- you" money and never be in a place to let someone else control my future again. If I was stuck in a bad deal or a job or a relationship, I wouldn't let money keep me from being resilient and saying no or walking away. Most of us don't do this in any part of our lives. Countless times I've heard financial experts say you should have at least six months of expenses saved for an emergency. Yet according to a 2016 GOBankingRates survey, 35 percent of all adults have less than $1,000 in their savings accounts, and 34 percent have nothing.[2]

Nothing.

Having savings is like having Wonder Woman's shield for the inevitable bad news that comes from pushing forward, taking risks, and facing uncertainty. This is why acting to deliver bad news is when your resilience is really tested. People usually have a tough time dealing with bad news. But I find that people have a harder time delivering it. They wait to tell it, try not to do it in person, stumble around it, and often fail to get it all out.

That's why I keep a deck of cards in my desk. I call them *candor cards*. When I give people one, they know what is about to happen. It's a shield because what is coming is going to hurt, and the card gives them a moment to prepare mentally and emotionally and not feel blindsided. Handing them a card also forces me to deliver the bad news with candor and kindness. I can't hide. I have set an expectation of what is to come, and I execute even though it doesn't feel good doing it.

While those cards are out, the person I am talking to can also feel free to speak his or her mind as I speak mine and nothing we say can be used against us. We get to the heart of the matter. The cards are my way of saying to myself: You *can* handle it.

So can you! You can fail and still move forward.

Really! Fail Forward!

One of the wisest things anyone ever said to me was that it is every bit as important to figure out what you don't like as it is to figure out what you do like. That's, in part, why we make mistakes. We're human! We're complex emotional creatures who often have no idea what we want, how to get it, or if we're doing everything correctly.

One of the best ways we can learn and get those skills is through experiential failure.

Failure is not only a part of life but also a really valuable tool for evolution and excellence when executing your vision. No one, and I mean *no one*, gets through executing any challenge unscathed—unless they just play it too safe. Think of execution like climbing the face of a mountain. No matter how experienced you are, you always know that something might happen—you could slip, your lead clip could fail—and you might fall. The point isn't that you will fall but how far and how prepared you are to accept it. This is why people learning to rock climb are told to make themselves fall: They need to know it *is* a possibility and what it feels like so they can get past the fear of its happening in less controlled situations. So go ahead:

> Get rejected.
> Fall flat on your face.
> Get the wrong seats at a concert.
> Fail every single day.
> Just fail forward.

Failing forward is a proven strategy—and not just for me. Think back to Elon Musk's story if you have any doubts. If you're not failing, you're not growing, and you're not trying hard enough. You can't expect to be perfect the first time you do anything. You're going to make mistakes. The key is to have a growth mindset and heartset where those mistakes help you grow, learn, and evolve. Like my IKEA nightmare? I truly believe that yesterday's "failure" is today's lesson that will lead to tomorrow's success.

If you have a system of support and personal resilience, the immediate feelings of despair will fade. Then you'll realize, in most cases, that failing was a good thing—even the best thing that ever happened to you, your vision, and your business as you execute.

Your team needs to know this too. When it comes to the people working to help execute your vision, you always have to ask yourself whether any lack of resilience they have is because they are playing it safe because they don't know how to handle things. Do you let your employees practice and even fail when taking chances? Do they constantly strive to know what they don't know? Why not let *them* do the same the things for a week that I just asked you to do?

When you do, you learn one of the most important lessons in parenting and business: **let them fail**.

. . . .

Do you let others test their resilience?

. . . .

It's a real catch-22 for anyone trying to be resilient in execution. Until you have the experience, you can't know how to handle resilience, but you can't have the experience until someone gives you the opportunity and incentivizes (or at least won't punish) you for trying to push forward. That's probably the best part about having entrepreneurial parents who refused to solve my problems for me. I learned to be resilient and act to follow my passion and achieve my vision.

This experience informs my personal motto that I tell my management team: *Don't blink*. Don't let the chaos around you affect you. Have confidence in yourself that even if you fail, you will be OK. Just keep moving forward. Your teams are watching you, waiting to see how you will react. *Don't blink*. In fact, it's in these moments—when heartset is linked strongly to mindset, showing the strength and depth of your resilience— that your leadership success is taken to an entirely new level.

Because when you do show resilience and grow as a leader, you understand that you need those people—those relationships— to help you execute and succeed.

RESILIENCE CHECK
Questions for Self-Reflection

Every entrepreneur, leader, and team on any field—be it sports or business—knows that people need to practice to improve at anything. The moment you get complacent about success or failure, you lose.

So how are you practicing being resilient?

What are you doing to set yourself up to effectively adapt to challenges and setbacks?

How well do you perform in stressful situations?

How do you handle rejection and deliver bad news?

Resilience—Trait Summary and Real-Life Scenario

RESILIENCE: REFLECTIONS AND MOVING FORWARD

- Failure and setbacks are inevitable parts of life and business.
- How we react to these bumps in the road has major implications for our efforts, so it is essential to know how to manage them effectively.
- There is nothing more rewarding than finding success by effectively adapting to challenge and setbacks!
- Manage your emotions: having a mindset that looks to find the lessons and the positives in any situation is an essential part of building your resilience.
- Teaching your team these same strategies for resilience will lead to a more innovative and successful organization.
- Resilient people are always in demand. They are inspiring— even stabilizing—influences when situations are intense or in chaos and obstacles seem insurmountable.
- You need to develop a growth mindset in which creativity, adaptation, and innovation can thrive.
- You need to develop a growth heartset so that you can cope emotionally with setbacks, obstacles, and crises.
- You need to practice resilience so you can better work through challenges, struggles, and failures when they happen.

- Be careful that your resilience doesn't leave you course correcting to oblivion or blind you to different directions. Remember: There are times when continuing might not be practical no matter what you do, and failure is useful only if you learn from it and fail forward!

BEFORE YOU GO: WHAT'S THE SCENARIO?

This scenario is designed to help you think about everything you have learned in this section. Please take a few minutes to complete this exercise as best you can. I promise it will be worth it. If you get stuck or you are not sure about your answer, go back and review the section. Remember, there is no right or wrong answer here—this is just a way of applying your new knowledge about resilience.

Often it is easier to give advice to someone else, when you're not wrapped up in your own world, full of all its complexities. A friend shares with you that a source of major funding for a new project has backed out of a big deal he was counting on. He is frustrated and stressed out, and he is talking about giving up and moving on. What can you do to help him?

How would you use the information you've learned about resilience to help him?

RELATIONSHIPS

Having the Right People in Your Life

Success is best when it is shared.

—HOWARD SCHULTZ

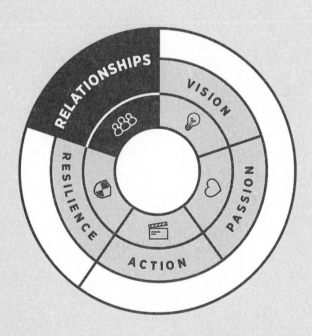

19

The Human Touch

The leadership consultant looked at me through the glass door of my office. She had been talking to my team one-on-one, and our eyes met before she spoke. It was clear she saw the tension in my face. I immediately knew she understood.

"Kimmo, you want to talk about what I found?"

"Mom, don't call me Kimmo at the office."

Unlike reports of helicopter parents of millennials showing up in their children's workplace to watch over or advocate for their children (yes, it's a thing), I have always welcomed my mom at work. In fact, she's usually there because I hired her. There's no nepotism involved. I hired her because my mom has and always will be my role model for understanding the importance and value of relationships—both personally and professionally.

Even if she does occasionally call me Kimmo at work.

Mom didn't graduate from college with a career path in mind. Like my dad, she was an entrepreneur but cut from a self-starter cloth: she worked well within companies. Her first job was running a new occupational therapy department at a hospital in Portland, Oregon. The director took a big risk hiring her straight out of college to lead the program, but my mother was ahead of the curve in healthcare with her understanding of what we now know as a "holistic" approach to patient care. She had a special gift when it came to working with patients with physical and emotional disabilities.

After five years, my mom left her job to start our family, returning to work when we were older. She decided not to go back to the hospital and instead found work in private rehabilitation, building on her hospital experience but with more of a focus on individuals.

Then after dinner with a friend one night, a new vision blossomed: a holistic approach to business leadership. Her friend ran his own business, and it had grown exponentially, putting him in the position of leading and managing people for the first time. And it was making him unhappy. My mom told me she could hear the stress in his voice, and soon after he started complaining about his health issues. He was blind to the direct correlation it had to his business, but my mom could see it. When she worked at the hospital, she listened to patients who had experienced strokes, heart attacks, and depression talk about how hard they were working for retirement and describe the stress it put on them. They didn't always see the connection either.

My mom listened to her friend's difficulties so she could understand the whole picture. The next day she called him at work: "I think I can help you."

The following meeting defined my mom's career for the next 30 years. Long before there was *StrengthsFinder*, my mom sat down with her friend and asked him questions to discover his strengths, passions, and natural abilities. She didn't focus on what he was doing or what he thought he should do. She wanted to know what he loved first, not just what the business needed. She needed to know his values. Thus, her first question that day, and for any other future client she would work with, was as simple to ask as it was difficult to answer (without reciting some line from the company mission statement):

"What are *your* values and 'nonnegotiables'—the things you will not compromise on?"

Your values and nonnegotiables are those few things in life that you will not make concessions for. They are guiding principles and beliefs that remain unchanged regardless of money, urgency, or another person. Your values help you live an authentic and balanced life—a life in which you are steadfast in what you say and do. Your family, friends, employees, coworkers, and customers need to know where you will not compromise.

For example, when my mom asks people what they value and they say, "Family," her next question is always, "How much of your time do you spend with them?" The point isn't to question their answer—she doesn't care what they chose—but to determine if their words are consistent with their actions. By extension, businesses that live by their values make it easy for their employees to make strong choices when up against a tough decision because they know they will be supported 100 percent, no questions asked—if their choices were anchored in the company values.

From her work with that friend, my mom's business evolved into team development with a clear focus on vision, values, and open communication. She was relentless in her belief that if people built on their strengths and interests to lead values-driven companies, then they would stay healthy even when going through major changes and transformations. Staying healthy: *that* was her goal in helping people love what they do every day because it taps into their talents and helps businesses maximize their potential.

Relationships Pulse Check

The following questions are designed to help you gain greater awareness of and to get you to start thinking about your relationships before continuing in this chapter:

- What are your values?
- What are your nonnegotiables?

Human. Potential.

We're all human so we all have potential. How much of it remains hidden or untapped in us? How much do we leave hidden or untapped in others leading to "people problems"?

I know I was struggling with people problems—my own and with others— when I started my first company. Yes, I had scaled it from nothing to a million dollars in revenue to a million dollars a month but . . . something was just not clicking. So I hired my mom as my mentor and our leadership coach to work through issues and the team dynamics that were difficult for me. But she didn't start with the team. She forced *me* first to talk about my strengths and limitations to understand what I loved and how my people could complement what I do, and *then* she turned the spotlight on everyone else. And her work with me started with that one question:

"What are your values and nonnegotiables?"

When I answered, "Relationships," my mom questioned me on how much time I spent caring for those relationships, whether I treated people respectfully and with kindness, and whether those relationships were prioritized in decisions I made. What I learned that day stayed with me, and it's why I brought mom back as we scaled. We are and have always been a digital company in a rapidly evolving industry. We pivot, adapt, and change every day. Days are filled with uncertainty, and sometimes we don't know beyond just a gut feeling that what we are doing is right or will work. But my mom showed me my North Star never changes, and that had to be as true for me at work as it was in my personal life.

My values that inform my vision are how I deal with a seemingly endless set of unknowns. My mom taught me how to approach every aspect of my life with generosity and a sense of abundance rather than scarcity. I needed to have a win-win mentality that flowed into every iteration of my business as I strove to execute and lift myself and everyone around me.

I value relationships above and beyond anything else—lifelong relationships that give and take, grow, and evolve. Those are the people who know the person you were and the person you are today. They have shared the experiences that helped define who you are and who you will become. Relationships at home and with my family. With friends and colleagues. With clients and other leaders. With the people who ask for advice or investment. With the people who work with and for me—because great companies must have great relationships too. And all of this comes down those two words: *human potential*.

There's no way I would be where I am today without all the people who have helped and supported me along the way. Many of those relationships continue to this day. By helping other people and learning about the experiences that made them who they are, those people in turn help me understand who I am and to see the world differently and more broadly. Which is why I say, I don't invest in companies. I invest in people—in relationships. I focus on people, cultivate them, learn from them, and grow because of them—both as a human being and as a business. The person who acquired my first company was a relationship that I had made a decade earlier when I was selling digital advertising at the tech startup that went bankrupt. My best friend from college is one of my most trusted advisors at work.

Those who understand and are aware of
the value and the importance of
relationships know they can achieve much
more together than they can alone.

Building healthy, inspiring, and supportive relationships isn't just a cornerstone to execution. It's an integral part of success in all areas of life. Because you can't do it alone. And to that point: Who wants to? We are biologically wired to connect with others, rely on each other, and work together. And of course, everything is better shared.

Great Relationships Aren't a Luxury—They're a Necessity

I know what I am going to say sounds obvious; everyone would say they know relationships are important. Same way we know sunscreen, sleep, and seatbelts are important, and yet here we are, still getting sunburned, sleepy, and hurt in car accidents. My mother helped me see how I got in my own way when it came to valuing relationships in the workplace. *What gets in your way?*

I find that often people feel they can "do it on their own"—or just find it difficult to include others probably because they feel they can do things better, faster, or more thoroughly themselves. Maybe you feel you don't have the time or energy to train or mentor someone. Maybe you don't know where to find the right people? Maybe you feel you aren't naturally a "people person" and find it hard to connect and listen. Does any of that sound like you? Simply put, whatever is holding you back from being other-directed, it's an excuse. Because when it comes to execution, success, and just being a happier, healthier, and kinder person, there is no substitute for relationships:

- In 1918, the Carnegie Foundation found "human engineering" was responsible for 85 percent of financial success while only 15 percent came from technical knowledge.[1]
- In 1995, the Center for Creative Leadership released a now-classic study on how an individual's inability to work well in a team and his or her poor interpersonal relationships are two of the biggest reasons for failure (the other being the inability to handle change, which we just covered in Trait 4, "Resilience").[2]

- In 2015, Robert Waldinger, clinical professor of psychiatry at Harvard Medical School and the director of the Harvard Study of Adult Development, revealed the result of the longest study of adult life ever done (75 *years* tracking the lives of 724 men): "Good relationships keep us happier and healthier. Period."[3]

Even without the supporting data, we all know the importance of having strong relationships in our lives to help celebrate our success and support us when we are feeling low.

In my experience, there are three key elements that are critical to great relationships in execution:

1. **Building a team and network around you,** including leveraging the talents of others and seeking out win-win scenarios
2. **Life audits** to help you minimize the impact of negative relationships and maximize the positive ones
3. **Maintaining great relationships,** fostering them, investing in them, and giving them the time, care, and attention they deserve—no excuses

Let's take a look at the relationships in your life through these key elements.

RELATIONSHIPS CHECK

Questions for Self-Reflection

Think about the relationships in all parts of your life—past and present—then answer these questions as a foundation for moving forward:

- On a scale of 1 to 10, how good do you feel you are at fostering relationships for mutual success? Why?
- On a scale of 1 to 10, how well do you distance yourself from people who are unhelpful or a negative influence? What holds you back from distancing yourself?
- On a scale of 1 to 10, how good are you at consciously attending to your relationships and planning interactions to maintain them? For example, do you reach out to others even when there's no immediate or compelling reason to do so?
- How often (always, sometimes, rarely, never) do you reach out to others for help, input, or support? When do you reach out, and when have you gotten help back? Why?

Now, turn the table on yourself. Ask five people whom you trust to be honest with you where they think you rank on these same questions!

20

Life Is a Team Sport

Have you ever watched one of those movies that have a scene in a school cafeteria, kids sliding metal trays along the rails of the line, stern-looking lunch lady in a hairnet slamming suspect-looking food, smiles few and far between? I was the lunch lady. Not literally, but that's how I sometimes think of myself when I think back to leading my first team in Hawaii before I hired my mom to help me.

Before my mom, it was my way or the highway, and my business suffered for it because the only one executing near his or her potential was me.

I'd like to say I came by it honestly. I never really learned the best way to run a team at the dot-com I worked at after college. No one there mentored me or led by example. No one felt they could take the time. I hired everyone who worked for me, but I had no control over my fate or the team's. No matter how many ways I found to make money with the resources we had, the company hemorrhaged more cash. Whether I was good or bad as a leader of my people was irrelevant; I still had to fire them all for reasons beyond my control.

When I started my first company, part of my vision was to have control over my life. Unfortunately, I let that need to control everything extend beyond me and to my team. And it cost me a lot. I'm not saying that what I said before was a lie: I did value people—I *love* people. But I got caught in the "there's my way and the wrong way" trap: I wanted things to be done the way I wanted them done. As a result, I ended up doing most of the work myself.

I soon found myself overwhelmed, overworked, and unable to scale quickly. Meanwhile, my team grew restless. With no incentive to do or go after anything other than what I told them to do, they delivered the results they needed to. The work wasn't bad, but it was not what any of us wanted. All because *they* did not own the work. *I did.* It wasn't that they couldn't do the work. It's that they couldn't be themselves doing it!

I denied any vision of their own, stifled their passions, controlled their actions, and left them nothing to be resilient about because they weren't pushing themselves to go above and beyond and execute on the highest levels for themselves, let alone for me. That's why I called my mom in to help. How was I going to be able to scale the company when I wanted to control everything?

Communicate Better

My mom spent time with my team and me to help us learn how to better communicate with each other and made sure

- We understood the outcomes I wanted.
- I let them feel like they had a stake in those outcomes they executed on.

- I let them execute—pursue opportunities and deliver results—in any way that was authentic to them as individuals.

The company soon took off. It was one of my most valuable learning lessons as a leader, and I often think about how much further we could have gone, how much faster we could have executed, and how many sleepless nights I would have gotten back if I had understood this one rule sooner. **It's okay if you don't get from point A to point B my way. The highway is big enough. There are plenty of other roads for all of us to get to the same destination.**

Be Accountable to Your People

Improving accountability involves developing relationships so engagement can increase, which is one reason why relationships are so essential to effective execution, especially on an organizational level.

I was fortunate to learn this lesson when I had to motivate 8 employees instead of 800 or I'd probably never have seen my family (or my bed). One of the most interesting points on leading teams and companies is that the challenges you had when you were small are essentially the same ones you will have when you are larger. The people problems I had at $1 million were the same ones my leaders and managers had at $100 million.

People can fail to execute for a variety of reasons, and one of the most important ones to be aware of is if they don't have the resources needed to complete the tasks at hand. One of the major resources in any business is access to other people—internally and externally—who can help drive execution. Whether it's experience or insights from another team or even another department like accounting or human resources, the presence of other people, especially people with skills and perspectives different from yours, adds accountability across a company. See things through new eyes. Hear things through different ears. Interpret problems with different skill sets.

This accountability is essential for execution in a world where distraction is everywhere. Even "time to think" can be a luxury, and speed is preferable if not mandatory. Yet, too many people and departments are in silos from each other. We may have open floor plans, but we have to learn to enable and value open communication—up, down, and *across* the company where people feel free and encouraged to speak up without repercussions.

A win-lose scenario is what is called a *scarcity mentality*: In order for me to win, someone else must lose. That might be true in sports, but in life and even in business, it's better if our actions serve an *abundance mentality* or win-win. Action without bigger relationships—and those that are dismissive of others—is almost always win-lose. Win-lose relationships are neither collaborative nor sustainable.

Leaders who know the power of relationships understand this. They have an ability to recognize the strengths and talents of individuals, and they are guided by a win-win mentality, always on the lookout for areas of reciprocity and mutual success. Because they know success is better shared and no one can go it alone. They know relationships are more than just leveraging everyone's time and talents to scale success. They are about give-and-take and understanding that this paradigm creates success for all, aligning everyone's skills and goals to execute better and achieve more. *They lead by building healthy, inspiring, supportive relationships—the foundation for trust on any team.*

You don't have to be an extrovert to build a network of relationships to do this! You just have to empower others to act in your stead. That said, there are three key ways to build, connect, and inspire the people who make up your network:

1. Get to know those around you.
2. Recognize and leverage differences.
3. Give yourself up for win-win scenarios.

Before we get into each of these steps to maximize your relationships, please know by "network," I mean *all* of the people you surround yourself with or connect with, not just those on your team. Often people are great at connecting with their teams, but miss opportunities to connect with those *outside* their teams, company, or even industry. Others may spend a lot of energy building their external network, but fail to focus on their internal team.

Both are important.

That said, don't let caring for and giving to others replace or force you to lose track of caring for and giving to yourself. We all run the risk of overusing our strengths to our detriment. Those who lead with relationships must be careful that the investment of their time and energy doesn't drain them too much or distract them from achieving their vision. Because you also have a relationship with yourself.

We should be invested in the success of everyone around us, but we must be careful not to overidentify with other people's goals and sacrifice our own needs for the perceived good of our relationships.

1. Get to Know Those Around You

If you're this deep in your execution evolution, fundamentally caring about those around you and wanting to get to know them better is the only way to build and scale your network and business.

When I say "getting to know people," I mean taking a genuine interest in them. You can't fake passion, and you can't fake caring either. The easiest way to do this with sincerity is to take the time to talk to those around you and find out what is important to them. And the best way to do that is to share your stories and *ask questions*.

The questions don't even have to be personal to start. They just can't be transactional yes-or-no questions like, "Did you have a good night?" or "How was your weekend?" But it's even better to ask questions that open people up like these:

- What motivates you?
- What inspires you?
- What are you passionate about?
- What keeps you up at night?
- Where do you see yourself in five years?
- How can I support you to get there?

I cannot emphasize enough the need to devote the time to ask questions and initiate conversations.

People reveal their passions in how they speak, what they value, what they spend their time doing, and, of course, whom they hang out with. They want to share that. Let them. If you're in a cutthroat high-performance business and the expectation is that you will perform constantly, then those performances are driven by execution. Execution needs that passion, and as you know, passion comes from a desire to suffer for what you are doing.

Are your people willing to suffer for you?

You can understand if they are by asking those questions but only if you actually *listen* to the answers. *Really listen.*

In fact, the two are related. We don't take the time to ask questions because we don't have the time or patience to listen to the answers—and even if we do, we rarely ask one follow-up question. How do you think that makes someone else feel? No wonder research shows that people who ask a question and then follow up with another question that shows interest in the previous answer are seen as more likable than those who just talk. But did you really need me or research to tell you that?

> Time builds trust, and trust builds
> great relationships.

If you find it hard to ask the right questions or ask them at all, try just *not talking*. Watching and listening to people engage with others reveals a lot too. Having this level of understanding about those around you will enable you to communicate with them better over time and inspire and motivate them more effectively.

Investing in my people and their personal growth, self-awareness, and development shows that I care, which in turn makes them happier and more engaged at work—a key to building trusting, intimate connections, communication, and mutual success. In fact, a 2016 Gallup study cited strong work relationships as a leading reason for employee engagement, a factor associated with increased performance and success.[1] The most engaged companies have four times the success than the least engaged companies.

Of course, you won't have time to invest in *everyone* around you! The key is to find those you know need you, who are integral to the success of the business, or whom you see a future with and spend more time with them. One way I do this in business is to focus spending my time with the five people who I believe will make the most impact on the company's success. The time I spend with them revolves around understanding their challenges, removing their roadblocks, and listening to and following up with their ideas. I'm constantly looking for those individuals who want to push the company forward.

Are there people you can think of now who need more time? Whom you could better support in their efforts to contribute to the team? Someone whose needs are directly aligned with your skills or values? Then invest the time—and set up systems that let others do the rest.

In other words: *delegate!*

One of the biggest hurdles to execution is delegating and then giving up control. Over time, I have learned that everyone who isn't pathologically lazy, always covering their butts, or constantly shirking responsibility is not nearly as good at delegation as they could be—including me.

To help scale myself and my vision, I've integrated mentorship and knowledge sharing into our culture. For example, we've used a "Buddy" program to pair new hires with senior people. This program ensures that each team member is engaged and learning from start, and teaches them about the people, the company, and our culture. We also have used an Ambassador program—run by the employees. This enhances, spreads, and cultivates the company culture and future leaders by providing additional opportunities for learning, growth, and knowledge. It's wonderful to witness our employees teach and inspire each other to take themselves and their careers to the next level.

But lest you think I use these programs and ask questions as a way to deflect sharing anything about myself, just ask me! Or rather, look around my offices. The walls are painted bright blue. Which will look familiar if you have known me for a long time: the bright blue is the same color as the blue polo shirts we wore in our family photos growing up. It's the same blue I have used as my company logo since my first company, signifying how family-oriented I wanted the company to be.

Although my company name changed with numerous acquisitions, the blue has been a constant. It reminds me of that strong foundation. The walls are an extension of me and my family— a reflection of how I feel about being here. They are me sharing part of my story and history. If I am going to be here and you are going to be here, then we will be a family that shares a vision and executes together, not just a company.

Relationships Pulse Check

What do you do to ask questions, share your story, and help others share theirs?

2. Recognize and Leverage Differences

In 2015, Google released data from its massive internal Project Aristotle study on teamwork, and its results were published in the *New York Times*. One line in the story caught my eye: "Success is often built on experiences—like emotional interactions and complicated conversations and discussions of who we want to be and how our teammates make us feel—that can't really be optimized."[2]

We can talk and talk about data, efficiencies, and productivity when it comes to execution, but how we make others feel when we execute is not a numbers game. We're all unique, and we need to treat each other that way—even in the office. This isn't about diversity per se but about treating every person as an individual who can help you understand more about yourself and others. Yes, including those differences brings big challenges, but it also has huge benefits, and I've found that the benefits outweigh the challenges.

We all bring different strengths, talents, knowledge, and experience to the proverbial table, and I've found it incredibly important in my career to surround myself with people who have what I don't. For example, I am great with numbers. I see them, get them, and understand them. However, I'm not as good in dealing with process or reviewing anything with lots and lots of pages and infinite detail like contracts or proposals. I get bored and start thinking about something else. That's why I made sure, early on, to always have someone on my team who is fantastic at this. In fact, not only is she good at it, she *enjoys* pouring over the detail. One man's trash is another man's treasure? True in life, true at work.

There are lots of great profiling tools out there like the Myers-Briggs, StrengthsFinder, and DISC assessments to help you understand and leverage those different skills and strengths. But don't let these or any tools become a substitute for actual communication. I've found that the more I understand about my people through conversation, the more we can recognize, nurture, bridge, and leverage differences to become more effective, productive, successful—and, ultimately, happier.

But be careful. If you want to get the best out of your relationships when it comes to execution (and really anything), then it's not just about your willingness to listen, as we just discussed, but your willingness to suspend judgment.

The Glenn Llopis Group surveyed more than 12,000 senior executives and their employees at hundreds of companies from the Fortune 10 down. They found the need to have a safe environment where no one judged was the number one thing employees said they needed in order to act as their authentic selves at work. Employees felt that without that safety, there was no incentive to do more than they were told. By more than two to one, they said that particular element in their work environment was *more important than feeling valued and respected or even trust and transparency from their supervisor.* Yet their *supervisors* thought feeling valued and respected as well as trust and transparency were the most important things. Only 12 percent of those supervisors said a safe environment free from judgment was most important—a real disconnect that's too common in business today.[3]

It was in mine. That's what I didn't say about what happened in Hawaii when I tried to control everything. The ultimate problem was that I didn't just make my people do it my way. I viewed their way of doing things as inferior. As a result, my team felt deflated, judged, or criticized. Because any time they tried a different way that worked for them, I shot it down. What I didn't understand then was my vision wasn't necessarily someone else's. They needed to buy into it to support it, but they also needed to own part of it for themselves. They couldn't do that around me.

············

How do you make people genuinely feel safe to speak up, be themselves, and express their feelings?

············

Today I am able to easily admit I do not have all the answers, and I do not judge the differences of the people around me. I trust my team to help me learn what I don't know.

In the end, the best thing about valuing differences and letting people be who they are is that they force you to put yourself in new situations to form new relationships and test what you know or don't. You can't keep telling the same stories and hearing the same ones from people who look and act like you and expect to hear something different. That leads only to confirmation bias, which is deadly for execution. If everyone is thinking the same way and looking for data to prove the same points, then tunnel vision takes over and new possibilities become impossible. All it takes is someone willing to see those possibilities, pursue them, and execute to overtake you. You want your people to be "intrapreneurs"—entrepreneurs in the service of the company's and your vision.

I want my people to be entrepreneurs and entrepreneurial, and so should you. You want your people to challenge you and push you. One way of thinking about things leads to one way of executing things. You need to open yourself up to and listen to multiple stories. You then need to let the people telling those stories leverage their differences as strengths to benefit the company and look for opportunities and ideas you may not have seen.

Even within a company that has more than 800 people, I want all of them to be individuals and feel they have permission to express their individuality. Everybody who comes to work for me today comes to execute on *our vision*. Tell me when and how you are going do something differently or how we might approach it from a different perspective, and I will listen. How else will I see all the opportunities out there? I know from experience that those opportunities are there, often just not in plain sight. But if everyone is like me, I'll never see anything but what I already see, just at scale.

Widening your vision with the perspective of others might even help you discover more of that unknown human potential in yourself and those around you. I believe one of the biggest factors in sowing seeds of doubt is underestimating your capabilities. You think you can't do something, therefore you can't. You'd be surprised how often this happens with even the most successful and smartest people I know. I had the CEO of a company I invested in call me and say, "Do you ever feel like you don't know what you are doing and you have all these people looking at you for leadership but you doubt yourself because you lack the experience?"

I said, "*I feel like it all the time. But I don't blink. I move forward anyway. And if I can, then I am sure you can too.*"

We are too often limited by our own minds. Sometimes we can overcome those limitations ourselves. Sometimes we need others to help. Sometimes that doubt can mess with your head. In fact, *impostor syndrome* refers to successful people who believe that they are not worthy of their success; they underestimate themselves and feel like frauds. Of course, anyone who feels that way almost by definition can't be an impostor, but the phenomenon is real.

It's not only another reason why you need to celebrate small successes and never give in to self-doubt but also a big reason that people who succeed have surrounded themselves with successful people who want their success to continue. At the very least you should always, at any given time, have a mentor, be mentoring someone else, and have a group of peers who are at your level with whom to share resources, cross-references, and gut checks.

Who is there for you?

Relationships Pulse Check

List the people you go to for advice and support. This might be an open conversation with team members or with a mentor who has experience where you need it.

I create fun groups of people and external partners who work together on a journey with me for a particular project. Take a look at the list. If it seems short or thin, make a new list of people to turn to and do it.

3. Give Yourself up for Win-Win Scenarios

As I said before, I'm constantly looking for win-win situations— areas of mutual benefit and success. In my opinion, you always want to be giving. For example, when one of my companies was running out of cash, we needed to secure a bridge loan. The bridge loan was the only way that the company would be able to have an opportunity of an exit, which we had worked for years to see.

But our venture capitalists didn't want to put more money in, and I had already deferred my salary for a year. I believed in the company and the team, but there was a very realistic possibility we would go bankrupt. That meant not only people being unemployed but also everyone losing all the money we had invested. So I loaned the company more money until we could secure cash to continue operations—a multimillion-dollar bet. Highly risky, but I knew in my gut it was the right decision for me, the team, and our clients so we could execute on the plan we had. If I hadn't done it, the situation would've been a lose-lose for everyone.

I did this knowing the risks, but I was confident I could execute the deal and secure the company's future if I had more time. While you may never be in the position of loaning millions of dollars, the situation brings up an important caveat in giving: you have to do it knowing your giving may not be reciprocated. You need to be okay with the fact that many people won't show the same in return. Not everyone believes in give-and-take. Some just take and leave you nothing to take back. But it's important to understand that an element of selflessness is integral to great leadership.

I'm okay with this, and you should be too. Please, don't give because you think it's going to be reciprocated. Do it because it's the right thing to do and you want to help people.

But when it comes to your team, I cannot stress enough the importance of empowering them to act on your behalf and the company's. I've struggled with this at times, failing to realize that focusing on helping others is making sure I'm also on the lookout for those who might be able to help or support me. *Make sure you have people that you can turn to for advice. Your relationships!*

Creating a culture of execution is all about empowering others to help you—to use their experiences to find those win-wins you don't have time to seek out. You don't want people just checking boxes, doing what they are told. You want to empower them to figure out how you and your company can best execute on the opportunities they see.

. . . .

If your people shoot for the moon and miss when executing, support them. If they check the box and miss, fire them.

. . . .

To do this means you must take *more* responsibility for execution on a global scale and less responsibility for executing strategies and tactics. Execution on a grand scale is the job of the leader first and foremost. As Roger L. Martin wrote in the *Harvard Business Review*, "Execution is the act of parsing out responsibility for those choices, making sure people actually *choose* (instead of waffling around in indecision)."[4]

Empowering your people to choose can be as simple as getting them to trust that you will support them when they act and not wait for the perfect moment (because it will never come). You don't need all the data. You just need to prioritize, have confidence, know I have your back, and do it. Don't get stuck worrying about the uncertainty. The only thing that matters is that you *know* you are following that North Star. The essence of effective communication is trust. People need to know that what they say will not be judged, criticized, or ridiculed. They know that their ideas will be respected if not always agreed with.

There's a difference between respect and agreement. When people trust you, they will open up. When they don't, they will shut down.

RELATIONSHIPS CHECK
Questions for Self-Reflection

One of the first things I do when meeting new people or interviewing potential new employees, CEOs, or entrepreneurs is ask them to tell me about themselves in five minutes.

Try this get-to-know-you exercise yourself with *two* people you don't know over the next week:

- What are their passions, interests, dreams, and goals?
- What keeps them up at night?
- What are the strengths they would like to utilize more?
- How do they spend their leisure time?

When you've completed the exercise, reflect! What did you learn? How did your increased understanding influence your interaction and relationship?

21

Audit Your Life

Ride your winners. Let them ride! Dump your losers. Cut them loose!

Investors have heard this advice countless times—and most research supports this position. Yet even the most prolific and seasoned investors ignore it. They fear losing their profits when shares are up, so they sell them; they hate losing money when shares are down, so they hold them. Not because they think things will turn around in time and the company is failing forward. They just hate the idea of losing money.

Of course they know better. You *should* ride your winners as long as you can—they're *winners* and winners win. You *should* dump your losers when prudence says quit—they're *losers*. Yet so many people don't, and they not only take money off the table by cashing in too soon but they also lose more money as the losers keep tanking.

What do you do? You don't have to have a stock portfolio to understand. Answer these questions:

- Have you ever held on to something that was worth less than when you started in hopes that things would turn around, only to find yourself deeper in the hole?
- Have you ever held onto something that was not worth as much as you thought and hoped the value would increase only to find the market for it—and thus the value it once had—was gone?
- Have you ever refused to get rid of something everyone said was costing you—and you knew it—but you still defended holding on to it?

Most of us—including me—can answer yes to at least one of those questions. Now try this. Ask those same questions about the people you surround yourself with personally and professionally:

- Have you ever held on to **people** who were worth less than when you started in hopes that those people would turn around, only to find yourself deeper in the hole?
- Have you ever held onto **people** who were not worth as much as you thought and hoped their value would increase only to find the value they once had was gone?
- Have you ever refused to get rid of **people** everyone said were costing you—and you knew it—but you still defended holding on to them?

Does that make you uncomfortable? It should! But those who master relationships as part of execution know they must surround themselves with inspiring, uplifting people and stay away from people and interactions that bring them down. Once you've got your team around you, you're leveraging talents, and you're creating win-win situations, it's time to make sure you are continually assessing those people *in* your network.

I get it. It's so hard to let go of *things* in our lives like stocks or a ratty old college sweatshirt. Now imagine how hard it must be to take the same advice about *people*. People we might still be passionate about and still have emotional connections to. People who once delivered for our business but not anymore. People who maybe helped us through, saved us, made us see the light once upon a time. But you must.

The most significant factors in your life are the people around you—your relationships. If you change nothing else in your life when it comes to execution than the people you spend your time with, you will have increased your chances of success tenfold.

Which is why every year I don't just take stock of the things in my life. I take stock of the people I spend the most time with. I arrange them into categories: those who lift me up and those who bring me down. The people who radiate positivity and energize, challenge, motivate, inspire, and support me? They're my winners! Those who ooze negativity and drain my energy? I would never call them losers, but they aren't positioning me to win. I need to spend less time with them or even let them go for now if not forever.

This process is what I call a *life audit*, and it is a huge key to optimizing relationships to execute at the highest level.

Audit, Audit, Audit

I remember the first person I audited out of my life: a close friend from college. We used to have the kind of wide-ranging conversations that always left me feeling invigorated. Sure we talked about the problems we experienced in life and at work, but we never got bogged down too long in the negative, and we used the time to try to solve those problems.

Then, things changed.

At first, it was only the occasional comment about a kid's teacher, a client, or our waiter. But soon enough, she seemed to be talking badly about other people all the time—people who were our friends! Every discussion about every topic seemed to turn negative. She rarely celebrated or led with the positive, if at all. Our conversations became, in a word, toxic—draining and exhausting, which in turn affected my mood at home or at work. I tried to talk to my friend about it, keeping things positive and asking if something was wrong, telling her that all our negative conversations were becoming too much to bear.

"Is there something you aren't telling me? Did something happen that I should know about? Do you really feel this way? Is there something I can do?"

I offered to listen and tried to steer the conversation toward positive and future focused topics. Nothing worked. I struggled with what to do. I wanted to be a good friend and support her, but the negative impact it was having on me was too great.

So, I audited her out. I started distancing myself from her, turning down invitations to get together. Could I have stuck around longer? Perhaps. But I reminded myself of the old joke: Doctor, doctor, it hurts when I do this! *Well, don't do that!* I was sure she was saying something negative about me to someone else as a result of my audit, but I couldn't worry about that. I had tried in good faith to salvage what we once had. It was hard, and yes, at first, I felt bad. It was not the easy choice. But this is where relationships need the power of resilience: you need to overcome the emotional connections that can blind or bind you to this toxicity. *We can't always "fix" bad relationships, especially when the other person doesn't understand something needs fixing.*

I resolved to let go of my friend to give myself more time and energy for those in my life who were going where I was going, who lifted me up, who shared positivity, and who saw possibilities and hope even in hardship.

Some of my friends think it's a little bit ruthless the way I toss out the negative people from my life, but I don't see it that way. Because it's not just about eliminating the negative. It's about accentuating the positive. Sure, there are *limits* to this concept and places where complexities and challenges arise. In these areas, it's important to look at setting boundaries:

- Familial relationships bring a specific set of complexities. You might have parents who are very negative people and who criticize you often, and you need to draw boundaries and limit the time you spend with them. If you have a toxic, abusive relationship with your parents, you may need to distance them from your life completely.
- You may have other family members who aren't always a plus, but you aren't able to remove them from your life because they are deeply connected to the people you love. You just have to minimize the impact they have on you directly.
- You could have friends, once pluses, who are going through extremely difficult times beyond their control, people who are dealing with such life events as an illness, the death of someone close to them, or even the loss of a

job. They need you and sometimes your positivity to help them through the negative. You need to keep them close.

- You can't use life audits to eliminate workplace responsibilities with people who are negative.

Simply put, you need to set boundaries for yourself when doing life audits. There is no way to eliminate all negativity from your life. But by bringing in more positivity, you can mitigate the effects of the negative parts you cannot control. The choice you do have is whether to have a negative or positive *attitude* when responding to others. *Staying positive is a choice*—not always an easy one in some relationships but still a choice to not let the negativity affect you. Choose positivity. I know you can.

Accentuate the Positive and Eliminate the Negative

Life audits are a powerful process to remove the negative *and* surround yourself with amazing people who allow you to step into your own greatness. That's how you hear the call of your own potential and get to where you want to go. While this might sound like the kind of clinical, right-brain madness a tech entrepreneur might come up with, it's actually a very heart-centered process! Through it you can create a more productive, inspiring, and emotionally fulfilling life.

That sounds nice, right? It's all about being active, engaged, and fully present in living the life you've got. We can't always control what happens to us, but we can control how we respond.

To keep us having faith that whatever happens can be for the best, that we are capable of amazing things, and in spite of what we read on social media, that the world is full of love, generosity, and opportunity, we need to focus on the right relationships. That said, it is never easy to let people go. In fact, it is usually hard and painful.

This is no less true at work, which is why we struggle with firing people who may be winners in some ways but are doomed by their negatives.

Most times, life audits are not black-and-white in terms of who is a positive or negative. I wrestled with this when I first set the process in motion at work. Running my first company in Hawaii, I felt extremely close to the people around me. Many of these people spent more time with me than they spent their families and friends. They were relationships that touched me every day and thus had the greatest positive *and* negative effects on me and the business. I needed to be honest about who had which effect.

Or consider this scenario: The third hire at a small startup I invested in was beloved for his personality by the two partners who had hired him as their sales leader. His humor and relentless storytelling got them through many long nights. He never sold much, but he helped them more than the bottom line, and that was important. But now that the company was growing, the very thing that had kept the partners going in the past was a distraction to the people who *were* selling. He had become a drag on the business, and despite efforts to reel him in and get him to focus, there was just no sign of change. They finally let him go. Unfortunately, they lost two talented people before they acted. They weren't so much lured away by better jobs or salary but by the inability of their leaders to address a situation that was affecting the culture and morale—a situation they knew had to be addressed.

Those leaders were blinded and bound to this relationship without any perspective for what it did for them, and thus they did not audit when they needed to. They traded better execution overall for blind loyalty to one person.

Now consider this scenario: A client had a killer sales executive—a woman who hit her numbers and usually beyond every month. Rarely did anyone equal or top her. Yet she had the exact opposite effect of the sales leader at the company I just described. While she built up the bottom line, she brought everyone else down. Her contribution to the gross sales was beyond compare, but her pessimistic behavior had a negative impact on the entire organization. She affected morale and in turn overall sales. She was a winner on the big board but toxic to those around her—no one wanted to work with, for, or near her. Her sales numbers in no way justified this, and after all intervention failed, she was fired in less than a year.

Those leaders were initially blinded and bound to the relationship for its gross numbers but without any perspective for what it did to the company overall, and thus they waited too long to audit.

Of course you shouldn't avoid difficult or challenging people or work styles. Often these are the people from whom you can learn or improve the most. I have tried to coach individuals who have worked for me in the past on how to better work with challenging individuals. I have also used leadership coaches, facilitators, and training and feedback tools so that we can better communicate as a team and improve as leaders, managers, coworkers, and employees. But too much of anything—like all the traits in this book—can easily become a negative you need to attend to in yourself or audit if it is in others.

If you are open and honest about what is not working and if you continually check in with updates on those areas and it's still not working, you can let people go knowing you did all you could. That knowledge diminishes feelings of guilt. Ask yourself: "Did I do everything that was in my control to help them be successful?" If so, time to part ways. You will still feel the loss, but the rest was on them. You can be responsible only for what is in your control. Then it is up to the individual to do the part in their control.

I challenge you to look at this closely and eliminate this negativity from your life. Letting someone go is one of the most challenging parts of business and life, and it should never be easy or taken lightly. But it's a powerful process that has been one of the keys to my success. Great people like surrounding themselves with greatness—talented people who make them better and who offer support, challenges, and feedback. Those are the key relationships, and they are not always the same year to year:

- Sometimes positive relationships take a turn, like that sales leader, and you need to decide if you are going to continue to invest in them or let them go.
- Sometimes negative people turn around, and you need to see that. For example, I would love to welcome my first audited friend back in my life if she became the person I once knew again.

Think of it this way: you're not rejecting people but rejecting their impact and behavior. The door can always be reopened if things change.

....

> Don't underestimate the potential of being with
> someone who demands the very best of you.

....

Being with people who believe in you and provide the strength
and inspiration you need to make your dreams a reality is critical
so don't be afraid of answering these questions:

- *How much time do you spend with people who deplete you,*
  drain your energy, or bring you down? The more you surround yourself with people who drain your energy or foster
  doubt, the less you are called to step into your **true** potential.

- *How much time do you spend with people who support*
  you, increase your energy, and inspire you to action? The
  more you surround yourself with amazing people, the
  more you're called to step into your **greatness**.

Relationships Pulse Check

Think life audits sound cold and clinical? Can't stomach
treating people this way? Chances are, you're just making
excuses and avoiding asking difficult questions.

Try this exercise as new people enter your life and you
look at them and the people already around you. Answer
these questions: Who strengthens you, and who drains
you? Who helps you succeed, and who highlights your failures? Does the idea of spending time with a person excite
your spirit or take away your energy? Then, decide who is
worth your time and who isn't.

Remember: Your time is your most valuable asset, so use what you do have for the people who bring out the positive in you. Relationships take time and energy to build, and they can therefore be difficult to let go of when necessary, especially if the emotional bond is strong.

Let's take a look at this for *you* right now and do a short life audit together of the closest relationships in your life.

These Are Your Relationships; These Are Your Relationships on Audit

One of the most enduring rules for business and life comes from Jim Rohn who stated that the people whom you spend the most time with shape who you are: "You are the average of the five people you spend the most time with." I've heard everyone from Tony Robbins (an acolyte of Rohn's) to Tim Ferriss repeat this advice, and I'm a big believer too.

Let's do it for your top five:

- List the five people you spend the most time with.
- Look at the names—really think about your relationship to them.
- Who helps you see the amazing world of possibilities? Put a plus next to them.
- Who deflates your vision or adds negativity? Put a minus next to them.

How many people have pluses? How many people have minuses? In my experience, the answer is generally pretty clear.

What if you have too much negative and not enough positive? Here are two tips:

- Proactively seek new relationships.
- Associate with people who are different from you.

Relationships Pulse Check

Having trouble with giving out negatives? Answer these questions: *Have you ever had to cut anyone out of your life? That was your first audit! What happened?*

Proactively Seek New Relationships

Seek out those who inspire you at work and spend time with them. Build a relationship with them apart from your direct job. Send a note, ask them to coffee, or simply approach them at a work event. Perhaps it's a mentor who has knowledge and wisdom or just someone whom you respect. Perhaps it's a colleague or friend. Maybe you can attend industrywide events or take classes on things that interest you to find new people. After all, in order to surround yourself with inspiring people, you have to find them to connect with them.

Associate with People Who Are Different from You

Find people who have succeeded where you have failed, and try to learn from their journey. Chances are, you also have something to offer them. Remember what I said about differences: while our instinct is to surround ourselves with people who are similar to us, it's also important to branch out and converse with people who may have a different approach.

That last point is essential to remember in our fractured political world in which we find it more and more difficult to associate with, let alone have deep bonds with, the people we disagree with. Remember how I said listening only to people who live, look, sound, and think the way you do in the workplace dulls innovation and execution? This is true in all parts of your life. You want people to test your ideas and beliefs and challenge your assumptions. The goal isn't to just be successful when you execute. The goal is to *keep* being successful—to keep knowing what you don't know and grow!

. . . .

Please do not audit people out of your life simply because you disagree with their points of view.

. . . .

Don't audit people who disagree with you. Engage them and let them challenge you.

It's perhaps more important than ever that we truly take the time to listen to understand—to make a concerted effort to get to know people as individuals and see the power in surrounding ourselves with people who think and act differently than we do. Not just for intellectual curiosity—though as an avid traveler, I respect that—but for building bigger networks that can tap growing markets domestically and globally.

Try at least to understand what others who disagree with you are saying by actually engaging them. Surrounding ourselves only with people who think and look like us only reaffirms what we already know. That's just another example of our keeping within our existing confirmation bias. That doesn't lead to growth in our personal lives. That doesn't lead to seeing possibilities and considering points of view that you might have never seen before.

Does that mean there will naturally be more conflict in those teams and relationships, because of those differences? Sure! And that is a good thing—as long as people are respectful and have the skills to handle situations involving conflict. If you and your team don't, make sure you learn the tools necessary to have tough conversations. Like an equation, minimizing differences just maximizes dissatisfaction. You want to create a workplace that inspires everyone to work authentically and to appreciate authenticity in others. That requires collaboration and cooperation— and tolerance—to address any conflicts head-on.

Questions for Self-Reflection

This time, your reflection is not as much a reflection back as a challenge moving forward. Expand your life audit to all aspects of your life. I challenge you to audit your life for at least 30 days.

Identify those people who support you, increase your energy, and inspire you to action. Then, identify those people who bring you down, deplete your energy, and are a negative influence. Reaffirm your connection to the former, and audit the latter.

This doesn't mean eliminate or ignore the naysayers from your life. Just distance yourself from their negativity, and see what a positive impact it has on how you execute.

22

Sharing Your Success

"Thank you, Kim," my colleague said, poking her head in the conference room before my meeting started.

"You're welcome! What's up? Do you need me for something? You're not part of this meeting, are you?"

We both laughed. "Nothing's up," she said. "I just wanted to say thank you for all you do and do for me and us here." Then she left. Just like that. The whole conversation took about 30 seconds. Thirty seconds to give me one of the most moving experiences I have ever had at work. No rhyme, no reason, no ulterior motive, no "Well, now that you asked, there is something I need." Just a "thank you" to let me know she was grateful to have me in her life.

There is always cause and effect in business and in life. What you put out into the world comes back to you. Maybe you've heard other versions of this line before. My friend likes to say, "Karma is a boomerang." A colleague always reminds me, "Do good, and good will come for you." Simple words backed by simple actions are very powerful.

My colleague's act of gratitude had the power to make my day: a simple act of kindness that made me smile through another meeting and still makes me smile today. Too many people create relationships when they need them or to get something accomplished but let them go when they don't. What happens then is exactly what happens if you don't service your car—change the oil, rotate the tires, check all the parts—to ensure that it runs efficiently and smoothly: it breaks down. Think about what happens to your body if you stop exercising or working out: you lose the physical, mental, and emotional benefits that you were getting from exercising.

The same is true about relationships: They need care and attention. Without regular maintenance, they can break down, too. As Professor Robert Waldinger said about the epic 75-year Harvard study of happiness and the power of relationships he led to completion: "Relationships are messy and they're complicated, and the hard work of tending to family and friends, it's not sexy or glamorous. It's also lifelong. It never ends."[1]

In other words, you have to invest in relationships—always.

I believe deeply what Paul Bloom, a clinical psychology professor at Yale University, said about kindness: "The key to the happy life, it seems, is the good life, a life with sustained relationships, challenging work, and connections to community."[2] For me, everything—every action and especially every relationship—is a long-term play. It's not just about getting a deal going or a project off the ground. It's about the chance to build new and lasting relationships. Often, this doesn't help me in the short term, but I know it will in the long term.

The long-term relationships are the ones who keep us going when our North Star seems dim—cloudy days and stressful times. Every one of us needs at least one person (a spouse, a partner, a best friend, or someone else) who supports us and is there for us unconditionally. Who won't judge us, try to teach us a lesson, or offer feedback unless we ask for it. Who will tell us it will be okay and pull us back to thinking positively. Who will always have our back, no questions asked.

Tips for Maintaining Relationships

In sustaining your connections to people, you must know what is needed to maintain great relationships that are authentic to you and make sure those actions are taken. Sometimes this is as easy as remembering in all the craziness of life to perform acts of kindness (like the woman who poked her head in the conference room) that brighten your day and the day of those receiving them.

Here are other tactics I remind myself to do regularly with all my relationships. Some of you will be better at these things than others. Not all of them will work for you, and none of them are easy to sustain in our time-crunched schedules. But gestures like these go a long way to making people feel acknowledged, valued, and nurtured. The key is finding a method that is authentic to who you are and works for how you live:

- Send a handwritten note of thanks or congratulations.
- Remind people you're thinking of them—and make time to connect!
- Don't make excuses about how everyone is too busy to be disturbed.
- Acknowledge and show appreciation for people at every opportunity.
- Include others "at the table" to connect.

Send a Handwritten Note of Thanks or Congratulations

An e-mail is fine if you must, but paper is best—even a text, as long as it is personal! But paper has a power that no other technology can match.

Remind People You're Thinking of Them—and Make Time to Connect!

I always try to call people when I'm driving, especially when I am on familiar roads or in an Uber so I'm not distracted. I know some people use that time to continue working from the office, but I use that time to reconnect with people I love first and foremost!

If you're in a crowded space, send a personal text to reconnect, and let your friends and family know you are thinking of them. Both my parents do this to me often (without the expectation that I will respond). It reminds me of the support and love they have for me.

Don't Make Excuses About How Everyone Is Too Busy to Be Disturbed

If they are real relationships, they will be thrilled to hear from you. I know I am. Think of someone who connected with you recently. How do you feel when you get an unexpected communication from them?

I got a call from a friend whom I've worked with on and off for years. When I picked up, he said, "Hey, Kim, I only have 15 minutes, but I just wanted to call you and see how you are and let you know I was thinking about you." He had no other objective or purpose other than to connect. I love it when this happens.

Even if I can't have a conversation with them at that moment, it means so much to hear from them.

Acknowledge People at Every Opportunity

This includes remembering birthdays and celebrating wins and successes with others, as we covered in Trait 2, "Passion." If you're not good at remembering important dates, make sure they're in your calendar.

But don't wait for that big moment to connect. Just as we should celebrate small wins, recognition doesn't need a trophy. I'm not talking about the workplace equivalent of handing out medals for participation that is ruining competition in kids' sports. I'm talking about what Ken Blanchard urged us to do years ago: "Catch people doing something right." Then, recognize them.

Include and Introduce Others at the Table

I'm always trying to figure out whom I can introduce to whom and connect others who can support, help, or work with one another. But while many of us are good at connecting people we know, few of us think about creating those connections around the table—be it dinner, drinks, or daily meetings—when we are there.

We tend to compartmentalize or silo people and teams ("Why does accounting need to be at the inventory meeting?" "Why does inventory need to be at the IT discussion?") or situations ("Why would I invite him to meet them—they are from two different parts of my life?"). The connections may seem incongruous at first, but if the people share the same values and goals, then being included feels great. Plus, a table is a powerful uniter of people. It's an invitation to "break bread" together and solve problems, create opportunities to build and grow the relationships you already have, and create new ones.

Relationships Pulse Check

For one week, reach out proactively and positively to one person every day. At the end of the week, ask yourself, "How do I feel? How has reaching out to other people changed my relationships?"

No, Seriously, Connect Now!

I challenge you right now to take a moment to think about what ways you could reach out to others and stay better connected to the people in your life. Not all of your relationships will change. Some conversations might not end as positively as they started (making the relationship ripe for an audit). But most will, and I guarantee that you will feel the effect this has on you. Because you need people—not only to scale your vision but also to create new visions that lead to bigger and better things for everyone.

As I said, the traits of execution are interdependent and progressive. We've gone from vision to passion to action to resilience to relationships, and if the progression continued you'd be back to vision. Does that mean you would need to create a new vision? Sometimes. But often it means an elevated version of the vision you started with.

When I started my first company at that kitchen table in Hawaii, I believed I would be successful, but I never thought I'd be where I am today. But as my vision and the company grew, I learned just how much I valued the relationships I had that got me to my first million and then the first sale of my company and then the next. If I had gotten lost in my vision and tried to go it alone—bringing on people only for the most mundane or temporary tasks and burning through them like firewood—I might not be at that kitchen table still, but I'd surely not be the global CEO and angel investor I am today.

At every point, I needed relationships—the ones that affected me and my business daily and the ones I maintained with no immediate need beyond a desire to stay connected—to grow personally and professionally.

I've seen the opposite approach to relationships too often. I had a choice to invest in two companies that on paper seemed to be completely equal. Both were led by dynamic entrepreneurs, clear in their vision, passionate about everything they did, deliberate in their actions, and steadfastly resilient. I decided to make bets on each of them. One of the CEOs was a team player, and years later his company had an IPO for over a billion dollars. The other company ended up selling for a fraction of that because the CEO never listened to anyone else.

It was his way or the highway.

There is nothing wrong with a visionary CEO leading the charge, but when you get stuck in your vision and shut out relationships, you can easily get lost listening to yourself. That's why you need others around you. There is nothing wrong with asking everyone their opinion on everything and ultimately doing what you want to do, but you must listen—and not just to the answers that you want to hear.

So I beg of you, when you reach out to people, *make it about them*. Remember the power of asking questions. Listen to the answers.

People who share their failures, successes, and experiences with you are the ones who can help steer your vision to more success. These are the relationships that balance visionaries who are inclined to keep their hands on the wheel and control everything. I'm not saying you won't be successful if you do not listen to others, but it will be a lonely existence, and the odds of scaling beyond your bedroom, garage, or kitchen table are slim.

I'll say it one last time: I would not be where I am today without all the people I've worked with, worked for, and have become friends with. Great relationships don't just help you execute. They will also make you happier and healthier! Think of them as your ultimate, crucial vitamins. What are you waiting for? Build your network, leverage the talents of others, seek to understand those around you, look for win-wins, surround yourself with inspiring people, and stay away from those who bring you down!

Good relationships aren't a luxury. They are a *necessity* for execution and success. And a rewarding, fulfilling, and wonderful one at that.

RELATIONSHIPS CHECK

Questions for Self-Reflection

If you haven't already, please take the time to carry out the actions and complete the self-reflection exercises in this section.

What have you learned about relationships and execution?

What have you learned about yourself in this section?

What will you now do differently?

Relationships—Trait Summary and Real-Life Scenario

RELATIONSHIPS: REFLECTIONS AND MOVING FORWARD

- No one would be where they are today without the people they've worked with, worked for, and have become friends with.
- You must understand the importance of relationships in your success by learning how to grow, inspire, and leverage your network.
- Open yourself up to a variety of perspectives and people building an authentic culture that encourages openness, individuality, respect, and understanding, and a sense of togetherness.
- Be careful to realize that the right culture is one in which people feel safe to voice their opinions without fear of recrimination or disrespect.
- Are the people you spend the most time with lifting you up or holding you down?
- Discover how to minimize the impact of negative relationships and maximize the positive ones using life audits.
- Find out how to foster and maintain relationships to help you reach your goals.
- Always remember: Good relationships aren't a luxury for execution. They are a necessity. And a rewarding, fulfilling, and wonderful one at that. Share your success!

BEFORE YOU GO: WHAT'S THE SCENARIO?

This scenario is designed to help you think about everything you have learned in this section. Please take a few minutes to complete this exercise as best you can. I promise it will be worth it. If you get stuck or you are not sure about your answer, go back and review the section. Remember, there is no right or wrong answer here—this is just a way of applying your new knowledge about relationships.

Often it is easier to give advice to someone else, when you're not wrapped up in your own world, full of all its complexities. Sarah is an entrepreneur, running a new clothing business. She's been trying to get her new business off the ground for six months. She has six key employees, and the company is growing, but Sarah is really struggling. She's working long hours. She's lonely and burned out.

How can you use what you've learned about relationships to help Sarah move forward and execute on her dream?

Conclusion: Creating an Execution Blueprint for Your Success

Congratulations! You've reached the starting point for executing your dreams. By now, you should have already taken the first steps to mastering the five traits and turning them into habits to reach the center point of the execution.

I just have one last question for you before I let you go:

How do you define success?

I define success as the number of lives I can positively influence. Since I think I can always influence more lives, I don't think I've reached my full success.

I believe in conscious capitalism and the idea that a business is a vehicle to change the lives of your employees, your customers, your communities, and the people you care about. I think that if we are going to be fortunate enough to be successful, we need to show that generosity and good fortune to those who don't have access to it. This is why my company volunteers thousands of hours a year to the projects we care about. That's how you create something larger than yourself that can grow and multiply and sustain itself long after you are gone.

That's legacy.

All that should extend to your personal life too. My grandma always told me, "Those who have the least give the most." Even if you don't have the least, operate from that principle.

My parents did, and I learned from their example. They worked hard to raise three kids while running their own businesses, and while we never had a lot, they were committed to sharing what they had. They were always looking for ways to help. Remember the kitchen table at which I made the loan pitch and where business talk happened every night? It was also a place where everyone was invited to come and share a meal. No one was turned away from my house. My parents even invited a refugee couple from Cambodia to live in our family room on a pull-out couch for six weeks. They didn't speak English, so we all communicated using body language, miming, and sound effects.

Approaching 40 years later, this couple is still a part of my family's life and community. The couple now has kids and grandkids. My parents' generosity taught me by example how we all have the power to change someone's life for the better.

In the end, you can build, sell, and profit all you want. You can have millions—billions! But dollars alone cannot be your measure of success. Please measure success in the kindness and generosity you show toward others and the hope you have for them. As you master execution and find success, make sure you define it compassionately.

Love may not be all we need, but the more we have in our hearts, the better our future will be.

That's your true legacy.

Acknowledgments

I am deeply grateful to all the people who helped me achieve my vision for this book from its first outlines to the finished manuscript to the final book.

Thank you to . . .

My husband John, for your unconditional love, support, and willingness to let me share the stories of our wonderful life together that are the heart of this book.

My twins Elle and John, for your superhero strength and for reminding me every day that miracles do happen.

My parents, for being there every step of the way to inspire me, support me, and love me—and always encouraging me to chase my dreams.

My twin sister Tracy, for being a great sounding board and remembering the childhood stories I had forgotten.

My brother Mark, for his endless support along the way.

Sarajane, for our lifelong friendship—we've come so far yet things still stay the same.

Sherry, for reading every draft of this book, providing great feedback, and making every chapter better.

Amanda, for being with me personally and professionally every step of the way for over 20 years—I am so grateful to have you in my life.

Liv, for helping me find my voice when I needed it most.

My wonderful friends, for your many years supporting my relentless pursuit of my dreams—it means the world to me.

My extended family, colleagues, and employees, for your continued support and encouragement.

All of my mentors, for your guidance throughout my career.

Chris, for encouraging me to always think bigger and for being my biggest cheerleader.

Heidi and Darren, for getting this published and launched—and putting such a powerful team behind it.

My incredible editorial director Donya and the entire team at McGraw-Hill, for producing such a terrific book.

The great leaders that I had an opportunity to work with and for—and all the companies I have been fortunate to invest in—for allowing me to learn from you.

And finally, for you and all my readers, I am so thankful for all of you—you are why I do this!

Notes

Chapter 1
1. Robert Kaplan and David Norton, "The Office of Strategy Management," *Harvard Business Review*, October 2005.
2. Chris Zook and James Allen, *Profit from the Core*, Harvard Business Press, Bain & Company, Boston, 2010.
3. Centers for Disease Control and Prevention, "Sun-Protective Behavior Rates," CDC.gov, https://www.cdc.gov/cancer/skin/statistics/behavior.htm, accessed December 1, 2017.

Chapter 2
1. John F. Kennedy, "We Choose to Go to the Moon," speech, Rice University, Houston, Texas, September 12, 1962, https://www.youtube.com/watch?v=g25 G1M4EXrQ.

Chapter 3
1. Erin M. Shackell and Lionel G. Standing, "Mind Over Matter: Mental Training Increases Physical Strength," *North American Journal of Psychology*, March 2007, pp. 189–200.

Chapter 4
1. Edwin Locke and P. Latham, "Building a Practically Useful Theory of Goal Setting and Task Motivation: A 35-Year Odyssey," *American Psychologist*, October 2002.
2. David Kohl, paper presented at the New Century Farmer conference, Des Moines, Iowa, July 10, 2012.

Chapter 7
1. Armand Mensen, William Marshall, and Guilio Tononi, "EEG Differentiation Analysis and Stimulus Set Meaningfulness," *Frontiers in Psychology*, October 2017, p. 8.

Chapter 8
1. Steve Crabtree, "Worldwide, 13% of Employees Are Engaged at Work," Gallup, October 8, 2013, http://www.gallup.com/poll/165269/worldwide-employees -engaged-work.aspx.
2. Thomas Clausen, Danish National Research Centre for the Working Environment, "Feeling Emotionally Attached to Work Leads to Improved Well-Being," *Journal of Occupational and Environmental Medicine*, October 20, 2015.

Chapter 11
1. J. Ferrari, J. Díaz-Morales, J. O'Callaghan, K. Diaz, and D. Argumedo, "Frequent Behavioral Delay Tendencies by Adults: International Prevalence Rates of Chronic Procrastination," *Journal of Cross-Cultural Psychology*, vol. 38, no. 4 (July 2007), pp. 458–464.
2. Henri C. Schouwenburg, "Procrastinators and Fear of Failure: An Exploration of Reasons for Procrastination," *European Journal of Personality*, vol. 6, no. 3 (September 1992), pp. 225–236.

Chapter 13
1. Innosight, "Creative Disruption Whips Through Corporate America," 2016, https:// www.innosight.com/wp-content/uploads/2016/08/creative-destruction-whips -through-corporate-america_final2015.pdf.

Chapter 16

1. Allison Schrager, "Failed Entrepreneurs Find More Success the Second Time," Bloomberg.com, July 28, 2014, https://www.bloomberg.com/news/articles /2014-07-28/study-failed-entrepreneurs-find-success-the-second-time-around.
2. Sarah Bond and Dr. Gillian Shapiro, "Tough at the Top: New Rules of Resilience for Women's Leadership Success," November 2014, https://forbusinessake.files .wordpress.com/2014/11/tough_at_the_top.pdf.
3. Accenture, "Women Leaders and Resilience: Perspectives from the C-Suite," March 2010, https://www.accenture.com/_acnmedia/Accenture/Conversion-Assets /DotCom/Documents/About-Accenture/PDF/1/Accenture-Womens-Research -Women-Leaders-and-Resilience3.pdf#zoom=50.

Chapter 17

1. Statistic Brain, "Startup Business Failure Rate by Industry," May 5, 2017, https:// www.statisticbrain.com/startup-failure-by-industry/.
2. Fred Lambert, "Elon Musk Says He Will Perform Same Tasks as Tesla Workers Getting Injured in the Factory," Electrek.com, June 2, 2017, https://electrek .co/2017/06/02/elon-musk-tesla-injury-factory/.

Chapter 18

1. Charles Duhhigg, *The Power of Habit: Why We Do What We Do in Life and Business*, Random House, New York, 2014, p. 129.
2. Cameron Huddleston, "More Than Half of Americans Have Less Than $1,000 in Savings in 2017," September 12, 2017, https://www.gobankingrates.com/saving -money/half-americans-less-savings-2017/.

Chapter 19

1. Charles Riborg Mann, *A Study of Engineering Education*, Carnegie Foundation, 1918, pp. 106–107.
2. Center for Creative Leadership, *Why Executives Derail: Perspectives Across Time and Culture*, Academy of Management Executives, Briarcliff Manor, New York, 1995.
3. Robert Waldinger, "What Makes a Good Life? Lessons from the Longest Study on Happiness," TEDxBeaconStreet, November 2015, https://www.ted.com/talks /robert_waldinger_what_makes_a_good_life_lessons_from_the_longest_study _on_happiness.

Chapter 20

1. Jane Miller and Amy Adkins, "Women Want Close Relationships at Work," Gallup Business Journal, December 14, 2016, http://news.gallup.com/businessjour-nal/199349/women-close-relationships-work.aspx.
2. Charles Duhigg, "What Google Learned from Its Quest to Build the Perfect Team," *New York Times Magazine*, February 28, 2016, https://www.nytimes. com/2016/02/28/magazine/what-google-learned-from-its-quest-to-build-the -perfect-team.html.
3. Glenn Llopis Group, "The Leadership Identity Crisis," http://www.glennllopis .com/research/the-leadership-identity-crisis/.
4. Roger L. Martin, "CEOs Should Stop Thinking That Execution Is Someone Else's Job; It's Theirs," *Harvard Business Review*, November 21, 2017, https://hbr .org/2017/11/ceos-should-leave-strategy-to-their-team-and-save-their-focus-for -execution.

Chapter 22

1. Robert Waldinger, "What Makes a Good Life? Lessons from the Longest Study on Happiness," November 2015, https://www.ted.com/talks/robert_waldinger_what _makes_a_good_life_lessons_from_the_longest_study_on_happiness.
2. Paul Bloom, "The Long and Short of It," *NYTimes.com*, September 15, 2009, https://opinionator.blogs.nytimes.com/2009/09/15/the-long-and-the-short-of -it/#more-7915.

Index

A

Abundance mentality, 218
Accenture surveys, 176
Accountability
  for action steps, 128
  for relationships, 217–231
Acknowledgment, of people, 251
Acquisition, business, 185
Action, 19–20, 159
  alignment of, 133–136, 137
  busyness as, 133–136
  disruption aiding, 139, 140
  doubt overcome by, 149–157
  empowerment aiding, 230
  fear overcome by, 145–148
  inaction compared to, 156–157
  as journey, 141–142
  necessities for, 155
  without others, 137–141
  without passion, 71
  procrastination compared to,
    122–124
  pulse check for, 124, 137
  rejection regarding, 118–119
  scenario about, 160
  self-reflection about, 120, 129, 143,
    157–158
  techniques for, 153–157
  trial and error for, 115–116
  vision aligned with, 132–136
Action steps
  accountability for, 128
  additional, 127–128
  difficult, 124
  doubt surpassed by, 150
  first, 114–120, 125
  next, 126–127

  obstacles of, 128
  planning before, 127–129
  resilience for, 193
  resources for, 128–129
  review process for, 129
  time regarding, 128, 152
Adconion, 49
Advertising, digital, 5–6, 7, 9
Advice, 11
Alice in Wonderland, 30–31
Alignment, 133–136
Alzheimer's, 81
Analysis paralysis, 115, 152, 156–157
Angel investor, 10
Apple, 116–117
Armstrong, Neil, 30
Arousal procrastinators, 122
Attitude, 238
Authenticity, 84, 207
Avoidant procrastinators, 122

B

Balance, 23–24
Bankruptcy, 2–3, 6
  loan preventing, 229
  of Pandora, 182
Best-case scenario, 157
Bezos, Jeff, 181
Birth, of twins, 166
Bloom, Paul, 248
Bond, Walter, 96–97
Bonding, 126–127
Boundaries, 237–238
Branding, company, 117
Burnout
  without celebration, 100–101
  passion causing, 95–96

Business, 38
  disconnect in, 225
  leadership, 206–207
  life audit for, 239–241
  vision as, 61–62
Busyness, 20, 133–136

C

Candor cards, 197
Capitalism, conscious, 257–258
Carnegie Foundation, 211
Caution signs
  of blind passion, 105
  father as, 58–59, 116
Celebration
  burnout without, 100–101
  productive passion fueled by,
    96–102, 107
  of success, 97–99, 100, 101
Center for Creative Leadership, 211
CEO
  doubt as, 227–228
  growth heartset as, 185–186
  hands-off, 138–139
  lighthouse, 101–102
  relationships of, 253
  responsibility as, 171–172
  turnaround, 44
Certainty, need for, 154
Changes
  adaptation with, 154, 209
  toward negativity, 236
  in relationships, 241
  vision impacted by, 53
Chili, love of, 37–39, 40–41, 134–136
Clarity, of vision, 39–40
Cleaning, stables, 70
Cold War, 29
Comfort, 193–194
Comic book, 132
Communication, 216–217
Companies
  acquisitions, 185
  approaches of, 253
  branding of, 117
  in closet, 193
  as family, 223
  growing, 8–9
  individuality within, 227

relationship investment for, 222
sale of, 10, 89–90, 166, 167–168
vision driving, 32
work environment at, 225–226
Competition, 116–117
Confirmation bias
  data cultivating, 139–140
  differences avoiding, 226, 245–246
Conflict, 246
Control, 216–217
Conversations, 220–221

D

Darren, story of
  action alignment of, 134–136, 137
  vision for, 37–39, 40–41
Data
  confirmation bias cultivated by,
    139–140
  40-70 Rule for, 154
  lost, 171–172
Delegation, 138, 222–223
Determination, 3, 50
Difference, 11–12
  appreciation of, 87–88
  confirmation bias avoided with,
    226, 245–246
  conflict because, 246
  of emotions, 86–87
  intrapreneurs regarding, 226
  leverage of, 224–228
  between president and tracklayer, 43
  in relationships, 224–228, 2
    44–246
Distractions
  in Hawaii, 8
  minimization of, 50, 53, 95
Dopamine, 148
Dot-com
  boom, 5
  bubble burst, 6
  emotions connected to, 77
Doubt
  action overcoming, 149–157
  action steps surpassing, 150
  as CEO, 227–228
  as rationalization, 149
  about scale, 152
  techniques overcoming, 153–157

Dream, 12, 13–15
  big, 47
  life, 7, 10

E

E-mail, 184–185
Emotions
  connection with, 77
  difference of, 86–87
  management of, 78, 186–187
  mastery of, 80, 148
  passion driven by, 74–75, 79–80, 85
  self-awareness of, 87
Employees
  empowerment of, 222–223
  failure of, 199
  injured, 184
  passionate, 92, 100–101
Empowerment, 108
  of employees, 222–223
  from entrepreneur, 138–139
  of team, 229–230
Energy, 235
Engagement, 9, 221–222
Enthusiasm, 83–84
Entrepreneurs
  empowerment from, 138–139
  parents as, 2
  role model of, 57–58
Evolution, of vision, 31, 32
Excuses
  procrastination as, 122–123
  about relationships, 211, 250–251
Execution. *See specific topics*
Experience, with failure, 199

F

Façade, 85
Fail forward, 20, 175–177, 197–200
Failures, 173
  obsession over, 98
  relationships regarding, 211
  resilience through, 171–172,
      175–177, 196, 197–200
  risk of, 151
  of server, 171–172
Family
  boundaries with, 237
  companies as, 223
  refugee, 258

Father, 1–2
  as caution sign, 58–59, 116
  passion blinding, 103–104
  as role model, 57–58
  sympathy missing from, 77–78
Fear, 8, 186
  action overcoming, 145–148
  of rejection, 118–119
Feedback, 62–63
Feeling, visualization, 46
Flow, state of, 99–100
Flying, 145–147
Focus, 8–9, 30, 178
Food truck story, 37–39, 40–41, 134–136
Foresight, 46
40-70 Rule, 154–155
Friends
  college, 235–236
  negativity regarding, 237–238
Future, 33

G

Gambling, 59
Generosity, 257–258
Glen Llopis Group surveys, 225
Glenn Llopis Group, 225
Goals
  growth after, 22, 23
  visualization compared to, 47
GOBankingRates surveys, 197
Google, 224
Grandfather, 44, 125
Grandmother, 7, 105–106
Gratitude, 247, 249
Growth
  from failure, 198–199
  after goals, 22, 23
  heartset, 177, 182–188, 192–197
  mindset, 177, 179–182, 192–197
  risk ratio to, 157
Guilt, 241
Guns 'N Roses, 192–193

H

Habits, 22
Hammock, 131
Harvard Business Review, 13
Hawaii, 7–9, 73
Headlines, 49, 89

Hearing, visualization, 46
Hidden Figures, 140
Hindsight, 46
Hitchhiking, 190–191
Horseback riding, 69–70
HuffPost, 180
Husband
  first step toward, 118–119
  sacrifice of, 89–90, 94

I

Ideas, 61
Identity, 41–42
Imagery, 45
Impostor syndrome, 227–228
In vitro fertilization (IVF), 164–165
Inattentional blindness, 79
Inclusivity, 251–252
Individuality, 139, 227
Infection, 166
Insanity, 125–126
Insight, 46
Intrapreneurs, 139, 226
Investment
  banking, 4–5
  40-70 Rule for, 154–155
  questions checking, 234
  in relationships, 220–223
IVF. *See* In vitro fertilization

J

Jedi, passion, 104
  self-care for, 105–107
  self-reflection for, 106, 108
Jeep Wrangler, 132–133, 189–190
Jennifer (surrogate), 165–166
Job, quitting, 115–116
Journey, 141–142

K

Kaizen, 119
Karate, 126–127
Kennedy, John F., 29–30, 44, 123, 140
KimPerell.com, 15
Kohl, David, 51–52

L

Las Vegas, 59, 101
Leaders
  execution scale of, 230
  relationships built by, 218–219

resilience of, 200
  sales, 239
  self-care for, 107
Leadership
  business, 206–207
  of team, 215–217
Learning, 83
Legacy, 257–258
Lessons, 11–12
Life
  dream, 7, 10
  work integration with, 91, 95, 142
Life audit, 212
  for business, 239–241
  delayed, 239–240
  guilt about, 241
  perspectives regarding, 245
  questions for, 234
  of relationships, 233–246
  scenarios about, 239–240
Loan
  bankruptcy prevented by, 229
  from grandmother, 7
  from parents, 1, 3–4
Love
  of chili, 37–39, 40–41, 134–136
  of horseback riding, 69–70
  as legacy, 258
  skill compared to, 72–73
Loyalty, 117, 240–241

M

Maintenance, 22
  acknowledgment for, 251
  congratulations note for, 250
  inclusivity for, 251–252
  methods for, 149–152
  of relationships, 248–252
  time made for, 250
Marriage, 9
Mastery, 13, 14
  of emotions, 80, 148
  of execution factor traits, 21–22, 24
  of passion, 75, 80
Meaning, 25, 40–41
Mentality
  abundance, 218
  growth heartset, 177, 182–188,
    192–197

growth mindset, 177, 179–182, 192–197
scarcity, 218
Micro-visions, 32
Milestones, 23
Mindset, growth, 177, 179–182, 192–197
Molyneux, Phil, 93
Moon shot, 29–30
Mother, 2
    business leadership vision of, 206–207
    potential maximization of, 208–209
    as relationship role model, 205
Mother-in-law, 81
Motivation, 1, 25, 82–83
Multimillionaire, 10
Musk, Elon, 183–185

N
NASA, 29, 44, 140, 184
National Basketball Association (NBA), 96–97
Naysayers, 73, 196
NBA. See National Basketball Association
Negativity, 235
    boundaries mitigating, 237–238
    elimination of, 238–243
    into toxicity, 236
News, bad, 197
Nonnegotiables, 207
North Star, 30–31

O
Obstacles, inevitable, 172
Onyema, story of, 145–146
Opportunities, 114, 151
    in difficulty, 176
    visibility of, 177–178
Ovarian hyperstimulation syndrome, 164–165

P
Pandora, 182–183
Parable, tracklayer, 42–44
Parents
    as entrepreneurs, 2
    generosity of, 258

loan from, 1, 3–4
in Portland, 57
Passion, 109
    alignment of, 133–136
    blind, 103–105
    burnout caused by, 95–96
    contagious, 71, 84
    cultivation of, 91–92
    emotions driving, 74–75, 79–80, 85
    of employees, 92, 100–101
    enthusiasm maintained by, 83–84
    as inspiration, 84–85
    learning influenced by, 83
    love compared to, 72–73
    mastery of, 75, 80
    motivation stimulated by, 82–83
    prioritization of, 93–96
    productive, 96–102, 107
    pulse check for, 74, 80, 86, 92, 100
    scenario about, 110
    self-belief driven by, 82
    self-reflection about, 75–76, 88, 102, 106, 108
    skill compared to, 41–42
    for success, 81–85
    suffering regarding, 18–19, 71–74
    transparency of, 40
    variation of, 86–88
    vision fueled by, 73–74
Passion Jedi, 104–108
Perspectives, 138
    life audit regarding, 245
    relationships bringing, 224
    resilience aided by, 153
Pilot training, 145–146
Politics, 245
Pool, swimming, 131–132
Portland, Oregon, 57
Positivity, 238–243
Practice
    of resilience, 177, 189–191
    visualization as, 46, 48
Pregnancy
    IVF for, 164–165
    surrogacy for, 165–166
    worst-case scenario after, 167
Prioritization
    of celebration, 99
    of passion, 93–96

Prioritization *(cont'd)*
time, 50, 52–54
vision, 52–54, 124–125
Proactivity, 244
Procrastination
action compared to, 122–124
arousal, 122
avoidant, 122
Progress, 133–136
Pulse check
for action, 124, 137
for passion, 74, 80, 86, 92, 100
for relationships, 208, 223, 228,
242, 244, 252
for resilience, 181, 187, 195
for vision, 34, 51

Q
Questions
for life audit, 234
for relationship building, 2
20–221

R
Railroad, 43
Reciprocity, 21, 229
Rejection, 118–119
Relationships, 21, 255
accountability for, 217–231
boundaries in, 237–238
of CEOs, 253
changes in, 241
communication aiding, 216–217
differences in, 224–228,
244–246
excuses about, 211, 250–251
during execution scale, 208–209,
216, 254
gratitude for, 247
investment in, 220–223
leaders building, 218–219
leadership regarding, 215–217
life audit of, 233–246
long-term, 248–249
maintenance of, 248–252
mother modeling, 205
necessity of, 211–212, 254
potential of, 208–210

proactivity with, 244
pulse check for, 208, 223, 228, 242,
244, 252
scenario about, 228–231, 256
self-reflection about, 212–213, 231,
246, 254
for success, 210, 211, 228
time with, 242–243, 250
toxic, 236
transparency with, 94–95
trust for, 231
as value, 209–210
vision expanded by, 252–253
work-life integration with, 142
Resilience, 20, 201
through failures, 171–172, 175–177,
196, 197–200
in frontline positions, 194
from growth heartset, 182–188,
192–197
from growth mindset, 179–182,
192–197
perspectives aiding, 153
practice of, 177, 189–191
pulse check for, 181, 187, 195
scenario about, 202
self-reflection about, 169, 173, 178,
188, 200
for success, 176
from twins, 163–169
Risk
of failure, 151
to growth ratio, 157
of inaction, 156–157
Rock bottom, 6–11
Rocky, 187–188
Rohn, Jim, 243
Role model, 57–58, 205

S
Sacrifice
of husband, 89–90, 94
limits to, 104
Sales
of companies, 10, 89–90, 166,
167–168
executive, 240
leader, 239
Savings, 196–197

Scale, execution
  doubt about, 152
  of leaders, 230
  relationships during, 208–209, 216,
    254
Scarcity mentality, 218
Scenarios
  about action, 160
  best-case, 157
  about life audit, 239–240
  about passion, 110
  about relationships, 228–231, 256
  about resilience, 202
  about vision, 66
  win-win, 228–231
  worst-case, 155, 167
Self-awareness, 87
Self-belief, 48, 82
Self-care, 105–107, 219
Self-limitations, 47
Self-reflection, 25
  about action, 120, 129, 143, 157–158
  about passion, 75–76, 88, 102, 106,
    108
  about relationships, 212–213, 231,
    246, 254
  about resilience, 169, 173, 178, 188,
    200
  about vision, 35, 48, 55, 63–64
Sendak, Maurice, 54
Server failure, 171–172
Shark Tank, 62
Sight, 46
Skill, 14
  love compared to, 72–73
  passion compared to, 41–42
Southwest Airlines, 194
Speech, first public, 113–114, 150
Stability, 2
Stables, cleaning, 70
Starbucks, 194–195
Success, 17
  celebration of, 97–99, 100, 101
  definition of, 257, 258
  passion for, 81–85
  path to, 15–16, 115, 121
  relationships for, 210, 211, 228
  resilience for, 176
  visualization of, 46

Suffering, 18–19, 71–74
Sunscreen, 23
Surrogacy, 165–166
Surveys
  Accenture, 176
  Glen Llopis Group, 225
  GOBankingRates, 197
Sympathy, 77–78
Synergy, 142

T

Teachers, Southwest Airlines
    recruiting, 194
Team, 212, 219
  control of, 216–217
  empowerment of, 229–230
  leadership of, 215–217
TechCrunch, 49
Tenacity, 3
Tesla, 183–184
Test, execution success, 15
Thinking, lost in, 60
Time/timing
  action steps frame for, 128, 152
  perfect, 152
  prioritization of, 50, 52–54
  with relationships, 242–243, 250
Timing, 60–61
To-do list, 53
Toxicity, 236
Tracklayers, 43
Traits, execution factor, 18–20.
    See also Action; Passion;
    Relationships; Resilience; Vision
  balance of, 23–24
  interdependent, 16–17
  lead, 24
  mastery of, 21–22, 24
Trust, 231
Twins, baby
  birth of, 166
  resilience from, 163–169
  survival of, 166–167

U

Uber, 190–191
Ultrasound, 166
Uncertainty, 42

V

Values, 207, 209–210
Vision, 2, 65
  action aligned with, 132–136
  alignment of, 133–136
  for America, 29–30
  as business, 61–62
  caution for, 58–59
  changes impacting, 53
  for Darren, 37–39, 40–41
  direction for, 31–33
  elements of, 39–42
  feedback gift for, 62–63
  headline as, 49
  idea abundance for, 61
  identity congruency with, 41–42
  micro, 32
  as moon shot, 29–30
  of mother, 206–207
  as north star, 30–31
  of others, 37–39
  passion fueling, 73–74
  prioritization of, 52–54, 124–125
  pulse check for, 34, 51
  reality of, 47–48
  relationships expanding, 252–253
  scenario about, 66
  self-reflection about, 35, 48, 55, 63–64
  simplicity for, 34
  thought for, 60
  time for, 60–61
  ultrasound as, 166
  in writing, 51–52
Visualization, 69
  goals compared to, 47
  as practice, 46, 48
  study of, 45

W

Wall Street Journal, 44
Walton, Sam, 40
Westergren, Tim, 182–183
Where the Wild Things Are (Sendak), 54
Win-win scenario, 228–231
Work
  environment, 225–226
  ethics, 73–74
  life integration with, 91, 95, 142
Worst-case scenario, 155, 167
Writing, 51–52

Y

Yahoo!, 5

About the Author

 **Kim Perell** is an award-winning entrepreneur, executive, angel investor, and the CEO of Amobee, a global marketing technology company with 21 offices worldwide. Amobee has been recognized as one of *Fortune* magazine's Top 10 Places to Work in Marketing and Advertising.

Laid off at 23 from an Internet startup, Perell began her journey as an entrepreneur from her kitchen table, becoming a multimillionaire by the time she was 30 and selling her last company for $235 million.

Perell attributes her success to her ability to execute, and believes execution is what makes the difference between success and failure. She is confident that execution is a skill that can be mastered, and actively seeks to teach it to others. Her passion to help young entrepreneurs achieve success has led to her being an early-stage investor in over 70 startups, 14 of which have been successfully acquired, and one that went public with a current market valuation over $3 billion.

Perell has been named one of *AdAge*'s Marketing Technology Trailblazers, *Business Insider*'s Most Powerful Women in Mobile Advertising and is an Ernst & Young Entrepreneur of the Year.

She has been profiled by *CNN Money*, the *New York Times*, *Forbes*, and the *Huffington Post*.

Perell graduated magna cum laude from Pepperdine University with a Bachelor of Science in Business Administration. An avid traveler (more than 60 countries visited), she and her husband live in San Diego, with their twins, Elle and John and their English Mastiff, Tank.